MY NEW JERSEY PARANORMAL PROJECT

RICHARD MOSCHELLA

We all shine on –

Richard Moschella

23

BEYOND THE FRAY
Publishing

BEYOND THE FRAY
Publishing

This book is dedicated to my beautiful wife and children. Mom and Dad, your son's a published author!

To all those who have gone before.

Also, for everyone who has helped me on my journey in the paranormal.

CONTENTS

ACKNOWLEDGMENTS

For all those who came before and advanced the paranormal research field. Your hard work will never be forgotten. Also, for those who continue the work for future generations of ghost hunters.

FOREWORD

MARCI KECK

Call it intuition or trusting your gut, but when I received a note on Messenger from someone I didn't know asking me to join his team for an investigation sometime in the future, it felt right.

Being the founder of the Picatinny Paranormal Research Society (PPRS) and having investigated several areas and buildings on the installation, I was invited by the Picatinny Arsenal Historical Society (PAHS) to do a presentation at the Rockaway Township Municipal Building on the findings in February of 2020. The large audience and interest by the PAHS members and friends and family opened the door to several new ventures, including becoming friends with the sexton at the Rockaway Presbyterian Church and the founder of the New Jersey Paranormal Project (NJPP).

Rich Moschella, founder of NJPP, reached out on

Messenger shortly after my presentation, stating he had not been able to attend but would like to invite me to join his team, which consisted of himself, Kim the medium, and Kyle, who did filming, for an investigation one day. It took until the spring for us to meet up, and we decided to explore Jockey Hollow. Being a military spouse, battle-grounds and encampments are right up my alley! I asked Rich if it was okay to bring my son along, as he and I do most investigating together, and Rich said the more the merrier. Hayden is twenty-seven and a big guy; I also wanted him there just in case this turned into a weird situation.

Hayden and I pulled into the parking lot early, as we always are, and moments later, someone in a van parked just a spot away from us. When the man got out, I knew immediately that this was Rich, even though we had never met. As we shook hands, I knew in my gut that this was going to be a good day, which it was. We had the same investigative style, and the same respect and curiosity for the history behind the locations. Actually, the whole NJPP team did, and the rest is history… which you are going to read about in this book!

As we progress through investigations, Rich and I are always telling each other to use our intuitions and trust our guts as to what we think we are seeing or feeling. Rich has started drawing pictures of what he sees in his mind's eye, and I am realizing that I am also able to visualize the person attached to the spirit we are interacting with.

Not only are Rich and I teammates, but we have become fast friends and can rely on each other to have an open ear and bounce ideas. With him I have found a kindred spirit, someone I know will always have my back during an investigation or even at 5:30 in the morning. So when Rich said that he was thinking about writing a book on his experiences and wanted my thoughts on it, I told him to trust his gut, and he did!

CHAPTER 1
MY INTRODUCTION TO THE PARANORMAL

I REMEMBER a story my father would tell about the untimely death of my grandfather in 1972. It caused many sleepless nights in childhood—but always piqued my curiosity about the paranormal. My father liked to start out by giving some backstory on my grandmother; he would go into how her family would have séances and explore the occult.

Just so that we're all on the same page, a séance is when a group of open-minded individuals and a psychic medium come together in a circle with the intention of making contact with a spirit. The spirit can be felt all through the circle, whether in the form of physical touch, temperature change, or other mystical occurrences.

My father remembers hearing his mother speak about one particular séance, where a spirit made its presence known in a very visual and active way. In the middle of the séance, the curtains in the living room began to sway, prompted by a cold breeze that gave them all a chill to their bones. No windows were open, and this mysterious breeze soon went away.

As my father recalls, the events related to my grand-father's death all started during a football game. My father was home watching football with his mother and father when they heard a noise, like someone walking up the stairs to their apartment door. As their gaze shifted away from the TV and focused on the door that these steps led up to, they suddenly heard a loud knocking. Startled, the three of them got up and went to the door to see who it was. No one was there. My father then went down the stairs to see if anyone had turned around and left. Again, no one was there.

My grandmother, who was sensitive to the spirit world, said that they should never have opened the door —when they did, they might have let something unwanted into their home. After some weeks went by, my father was arriving home to his parents' apartment. He was in the process of parking his car when he looked up at their apartment window and noticed a dark figure looking out with the light on. He got out of his car and went up the stairs—only to see that the lights were all off, and his mother and father were both in bed sleeping.

About two or three o'clock in the morning, my father awoke to a loud moaning and groaning, like someone was in horrible pain. There was a bar downstairs from the apartment, and my father quickly went to his window and opened it to make sure no one was hurt. As he peered out, nothing was to be seen. The sidewalk below was empty, and nothing outside could have been causing these horrible noises. When he closed his window, the night air seemed heavier than usual. That was when he realized that the moaning was not coming from outside, but from his sister's bedroom.

My father rushed into his sister's room and found his mother sleeping there. (That wasn't unusual. If my grandmother had trouble sleeping, she would sleep in her daughter's bedroom for a change.) He grabbed his mother's arm and tried to wake her, wanting to make sure she was okay. When she woke up, she refused to tell my father what she saw in her dream—a dream that was causing such horrible emotions and pain. To my father's shock, my grandfather slept through the entire night's commotion and never heard a sound.

My grandmother remained shaken. Over the following days, she could not hold back her memories of that horrible dream. Here is the account she shared with my father.

In the dream, her mother, who had been dead for at least fifteen years, came to her and stood next to the bed. As she looked up at this ghostly image of her long-departed mother, she decided to grab hold of her arm. It was cold and clammy. As she touched her dead mother's arm, she felt a slimy residue—yet her grasp went right through it.

My grandmother would have another visit by her mother's spirit that did not last as long as the first encounter. During this second visit, my grandmother mustered the courage to try to reach in the direction of the ghostly form as it stood next to the bed. My father heard the noises coming from the bedroom, rushed in, and found my grandmother in a cold sweat. She exhaled and said, "She came back."

Once again, my grandfather didn't hear any of the

commotion. When told about what had happened for a second time, he dismissed it. In the following days, he teased my grandmother, saying that she'd lost her mind.

Another few days passed, and my grandmother could see something was not right in my grandfather's face; he had a very troubled look about him. When she asked him if everything was okay, he admitted that he had a terrible dream but didn't want to talk about it. He wanted to leave it at that and not relive whatever he'd encountered.

My father remembers the fateful morning of his father's death. Like he normally did, my grandfather kissed my grandmother goodbye, then grabbed all the supplies he needed for that day's work as a truck driver and left. My grandmother was scheduled for jury duty and getting ready to leave the apartment. Suddenly, the plates in the cabinets started to shake, the lights flickered, and a chandelier swayed violently back and forth. She was so scared.

After pulling herself together, my grandmother went to jury duty, thinking about what had happened in the apartment that morning and her horrible dreams. She was trying to figure out what all this could mean and if there was a message behind any of it.

When the morning turned into the afternoon, my grandmother received the phone call no wife ever wants to get. The voice on the phone informed her that her husband had been killed in an accident. According to some reports, he had gotten out of his truck and was crushed from the waist up by another passing vehicle. Some unknown witnesses said they saw him getting into a fight with a group of men. There are many stories surrounding his death.

Over the years, our family has come to accept that we will never fully know what happened that morning in Hudson County, New Jersey. But in the months after the death of her husband, my grandmother came to her own conclusion about the two times her deceased mother came to her. My grandfather was the only one in the apartment who never heard her screaming and moaning; he remained fast asleep.

My grandmother felt that her mother was coming to her and trying to warn her about what was going to happen to her husband. She spent the rest of her life retelling this story. My father told it to me. And now it is my turn to tell it to you.

This was the story that started my research into the paranormal. What made it especially fascinating to me is the fact that it was personal. Not only were all the witnesses close family members, but so was the spirit. From that moment on, I began to consume books on the paranormal and watch everything I could on the subject. I was on a mission for information about this unseen world and wanted to understand more about communication with its inhabitants.

In 2004, I went along with a friend who was having a reading at a medium's home. As we walked up to the door and rang the bell, I felt this weird sensation across my shoulders—it felt like electricity. It also felt like when you're in line at a store and someone is standing way too close behind you.

The medium answered the door, and we both walked into the living room. Since this reading was for my friend, I was just going to wait in the living room. The medium went upstairs to prepare for the reading and, a few moments later, came down to where we were sitting in the living room. She told my friend that before she could continue and conduct her reading with him, she needed to speak to me.

Looking over my head, she began to tell me that a man was with me. "He's dressed like a truck driver," she continued. "He wants to recognize the 'JR' and wants to let you know he's very proud of you."

I was speechless. My grandfather was killed driving a truck, and I am Richard Moschella Jr. Since I never met him, I had often wondered if my grandfather was proud of my accomplishments. He wanted to come and get those messages across. The medium then started a reading for my friend, and my communication was over.

I drove home that night feeling overwhelmed with

emotions and grief for the grandfather I never got the chance to know. But somehow, through the help of a caring medium, we had a conversation that meant so much. I knew that we would get the opportunity to connect again, all in due time.

CHAPTER 2
KNOW THE LOCATION

Presbyterian Church. Rockaway Township, New Jersey

WHEN SELECTING LOCATIONS FOR NJPP, I find it vital for spirit communication to understand the location's history. These locations build up so many layers of spirit activity; as investigators, we need to be able to distinguish the evidence we are getting. It's common to get spirits from different time periods communicating at the same time. Having a list of the names and time periods of the people who lived at the location you're investigating is critical. Cemetery records help. Also, websites like Find A Grave are great to get information to help confirm who's communicating with you.

You can also take a deeper dive into your paranormal investigation by paying a visit to your local library or scheduling an appointment with the area's local historian. All these resources can really improve your results and make communicating with the spirits as easy as possible.

THE WORKBENCH

It was the summer of 2007, and I had just moved into an apartment in Little Falls, New Jersey. It was your typical basement apartment. When the owners of the home moved in, they had renovated the basement with the focus on renting the space for extra income. As the workers began to knock down walls and remove items left behind by the previous owners, they discovered an old wooden workbench along the back wall. The workbench was almost frozen in time and still had items stored in its drawers. One drawer contained old screws; another held a few tubs of old wood glue. On its surface sat an old level and a wood measuring stick. There was also an old baseball hat that hung on a wooden peg.

When the workers started to dismantle the workbench, it did not take long to come crashing down. A few shots from a hammer and what had once served the past homeowner as a place he worked so hard was destroyed.

The basement apartment took a few weeks to get ready to be rented. When it was done, you would have never known that it had been a humble workspace and that an old workbench had lined its back wall. It was beautifully renovated and even had a large egress window that let so much natural light into the once dark basement.

I moved in, and a few weeks went by, then I started to notice some strange occurrences. When the owners would be out and no one was home upstairs, I would hear walking. I heard something fall on the floor above my bedroom in the middle of the night—again, no one was home upstairs. The owners were in their sixties and spent a lot of time down the shore or at Atlantic City. It was great that I had the entire property almost to myself, but something else was starting to spend time with me. Something I could not see, but that certainly was making its presence known.

I went to a metaphysical store a few towns away and

purchased a bundle of sage and returned with a small vial of holy water. I wanted to see if I could cleanse the home myself and get whatever was in there out. When I returned to the basement apartment, a picture frame that had hung over my kitchen sink was slammed facedown on the living room floor. It was a good ten feet away from where it had hung. I was in total shock. I knew at that moment that whatever was haunting this home was very upset at something.

When I mentioned what had been happening to the owners, I learned that they also were having strange things happen on their floor. The wife would see a shadow move from the corner of her eye from time to time and also hear low voices talking in rooms of the house. The husband would just have an uneasy feeling in certain rooms of the house. I was unsettled but also in a way relieved to know that my landlords were having these experiences too.

The wife informed me that they would be having a medium over for a small group, and they would ask her if she picked up on anything haunting the home. The day came for the medium to visit and perform a few readings for the homeowners' close friends. Once the medium walked into the upstairs living room, she could not hold back what she was hearing and feeling from the spirit in the home.

The medium began to say that the spirit of the man

who used to live there still felt like the owner of the property and was extremely upset about the changes that were made to *his* home. He was especially angry that his workbench had been destroyed and thrown away by the workers. He was also not happy to have someone living in his basement space.

The medium conveyed to the spirit that the home was no longer his, and we had the home's best interest in mind with the renovations that were done. She also explained that we were sorry that the workbench was no longer there, and I was open to letting him stay if he stopped trying to scare us.

After the medium's visit, the activity in the basement did get better, which made me think about renovations and the impact they have not only on the living but the dead. I moved out a few years later. To this day, I often wonder about the new owners of the home in Little Falls, and if they ever experience the workbench spirit.

CHAPTER 3
VOICES

Tombstone. Ringwood Manor Cemetary.

EXCUSE You

I was sitting in a friend's kitchen one night, having a few beers and watching a baseball game. My friend let out a deep beer burp that was quite impressive in its baritone sound. Immediately after, we heard this strange, robotic-like voice that sounded as if it was right next to us. This voice simply said, "Excuse you." We both looked at each other and called it a night. The voice sounded like it was coming from all around us and from some invisible presence in the room. I will never forget how clear the spirit's voice was and how it clearly cared about having good manners.

MY HUSBAND'S Name Is Frank

I was honored to listen to a tape recording of a friend's reading with a medium. What made this reading so astounding: when the tape was played back, her deceased grandmother's voice could be heard. The medium told my friend that her grandmother had a message for her living husband. You hear the medium ask the grandmother's spirit, "What is your husband's name?" When the tape is played back, you hear a woman's voice say, "My husband's name is Frank. My husband's name is Frank." Then the medium turned to my friend and said, "Your grandfather's name is Frank." My friend was blown away because the voice that came through on the tape sounded just like her grandmother. The reading not only helped ease her grief over the loss of her grandmother, but also let her know that we do not die. It was such a powerful reading and confirmation on spirit communication

THE CLOSET

I rented an apartment in Elmwood Park, New Jersey, and again noticed paranormal activity happening in the home. It was on the second floor of a two-family house located just off Market Street. The home was owned by a single older woman who was usually in bed early and did not have much company. One night as I was lying on the couch in the living room, I heard footsteps walking up the wooden stairs towards the door to my apartment. When I went to the door to see who was there, I was shocked to see no one.

Another time I came home and all the cabinets in the kitchen were left open. Occurrences like these would just keep happening. Then late one night, I was lying down in the bedroom and watching TV. The master bedroom had a walk-in closet at the foot of the bed that was very spacious. Around one o'clock in the morning, I suddenly heard talking coming from the closet. The talking sounded muffled, like two people having an argument with their hands over their mouths. I quickly turned off the television and listened more closely. Though I could not make out the words, I heard the muffled exchange continue. Once it stopped, for my own satisfaction, I went downstairs to see if any lights were on and if everything was okay with the owner. The bottom floor of the house was completely dark, and not a sound could be heard.

In the coming months, there would be more conversations from the closet as well as mysterious noises and happenings throughout the house. The cabinets continued to open by themselves all the way up until I moved. I wonder if this apartment is still an active location after all these years.

REFLECTION

In childhood I remember countless times going to bed at night and hearing footsteps and even feeling something pressing down on the bed I was sleeping in. These memories would come back to me when I experienced similar paranormal events in adult life. I thought to myself, "Could something be following me to every place I move?" It wasn't until my mid-twenties that I had a highly respected medium confirm I have the ability to connect with spirits and I probably already had. The medium went on to tell me about classes I could take to sharpen my abilities. There were also meditations that I could do to awaken the gift.

I began to immerse myself in books on the subject written by John Holland, Hans Holzer, Jane Doherty, Jeffrey Wands, Michelle Belanger, James Van Praagh,

John Edward, Raymond Moody, George Anderson, Jason Hawes and Grant Wilson, Ed and Lorraine Warren, Chip Coffey, Janet Nohavec, Sonia Choquette, and Colette Baron-Reid to name a few. If you are looking to expand your knowledge of the spirit world or believe you have the gift too, I strongly suggest reading books by these authors; in my opinion, they are must for your education.

We are so lucky to live in an age where information is everywhere, and we have access to tons of webinars, podcasts, seminars, and lectures all at our fingertips. Just a decade ago, it was so much harder to get exposed to this information. We are truly living in an age of spirit enlightenment. The teachers have emerged, and they are willing to help guide you on your personal journey.

CHAPTER 4
WHY SPIRITS STAY

Inside Presbyterian Church, Rockaway Township,
New Jersey

WHY DO spirits stay in the places they lived or died on earth? That's the million-dollar question, and to be totally honest, I don't have absolute proof to show you why. We only have theories from researchers in the paranormal field that have explored this age-old question. It's a hard question, particularly if you were brought up with a common religious belief about happens when we die: if you were a good person, you get to go up to heaven, and if you were a bad person, you would go down to hell.

I was brought up in a Catholic family that only stepped into church for weddings, funerals and the occasional childhood rite of passage in receiving sacraments. Not being such a devout Catholic gave me a freedom to explore different beliefs, especially in the metaphysical world. I devoured books on reincarnation and past life experiences and life after death communication. Through these books, I got an understanding of the journey of the soul after life ends here on earth.

POSSESSIONS

Can people's earthly possessions have a spirit or spirits attached to them? Yes, is what I believe. I have been on enough investigations to tell you we have gotten too much evidence around objects that people used in life. This is similar to the belief in places drawing spirit energy back once human death occurs. I find that objects can also hold a connection to a spirit. Most of the time, the connection is harmless but, in some cases, darker energy can be infused in these objects. When it comes to the darker energy experts in the paranormal field, John Zaffis has written many great books on haunted objects.

I have been in so many historical homes and gotten great responses around items that were used in everyday life and even items used for military purposes. Imprinted emotions and spirits are usually attached to these and are not negative. It's important to treat these items when being investigated with absolute respect and honor. These objects meant something to someone and played a part in their life, so it's our job as investigators to honor their memory and try to make a connection with the spirit.

————

PLACES

I believe some spirits are attached to the locations they took to fondly in life. Once human death occurs, they choose to stay behind and inhabit these spaces. This makes sense to me from the locations we visited and communicated with the spirit inhabitants. I also think that the spirit might not always be at the location; since a spirit is energy, it can be at many places at the same time or choose to be entirely at one location. A spirit can be a thought away and choose to make itself present.

In some cases, spirits can be attached to the land itself; we still find locations where Native American

23

spirits come through to communicate. Long before the settlers arrived in the Americas, the land was inhabited by indigenous tribes that worshiped the land and what it offered. It provided food, shelter and protection to these native tribes. Their spirits are still very much around in the obvious places we investigate, like state parks and places located in the wilderness of New Jersey.

We also have found Native American spirits in places you would walk by every day and not even think you could encounter them.

I can imagine if something were to happen to me and my life was cut short for some reason, I would like to stick around and watch my children grow up. There would be that feeling of not wanting to leave my family's side and to still be around the people I love. I believe this can be the same reason most spirits stick around on the earth plane and don't move on. For some reason, they are attached to or have times in this realm that they can't let go of in death. We have no idea how time is affected in the spirit world. Who knows? One hundred years in earth time could fly by in the blink of an eye in the spirit realm. Time might not exist at all, but I will leave that up to the experts to debate.

SUDDEN OR TRAGIC Death

Then there are the lives that were cut short due to illness or accident. These cases are emotionally grueling because of how these people passed and the lives that were affected by the tragedy. I have seen responses from spirits in some of these untimely cases just wanting to confirm they are okay on the other side and help a family member who is grieving. There have also been cases of a spirit not knowing they have died, or they choose to stay behind. Whether it's unfinished business or denial, these souls had an abrupt end of life on the earth plane. In some communications, they can come across angry because of their refusal to accept their own death.

An investigator must have empathy for and patience with spirits like these. It could take many return trips to the location to build a foundation of trust and perhaps eventually let them move on by telling their story.

So what makes a spirit stay on the earth plane? The ultimate answer, I believe, is human emotion—the desire of not letting go and, at times, fear of not knowing what happens next.

CHAPTER 5
WATERLOO VILLAGE

Taken in Waterloo Village, New Jersey

THE LITTLE GIRL

It was late October 2020 when the New Jersey Paranormal Project decided to investigate Waterloo Village. Waterloo Village is a nineteenth-century restored village that covers the time frame from a four-hundred-year-old

Lenape Indian village to a bustling port along the once prosperous Morris Canal. The village is a working mill complex with gristmills and sawmills, a general store, blacksmith shop, and several historic houses where it appears that time has stood still.

When I started my research on the area, I came across a book by paranormal investigator Eleanor Wagner called *Sussex County Hauntings*. It features a section devoted to the encounters people have had over the years at Waterloo Village.

I reached out to Eleanor and her group, the Lady Ghostbusters, and invited them to join NJPP and myself for an investigation of Waterloo Village. When the teams arrived at the location that October morning, you could feel the stillness from the night fading as the sun began to climb above the fall color trees.

Autumn in New Jersey is an amazing experience, especially at these historical sites. The morning fog danced on the water's surface and, for a few fleeting seconds, looked like ghostly fingers reaching up from the water towards the sky.

We began our investigation at a mill on the water's edge, and immediately started to pick up on spirits. We had two mediums, Maryann Taylor and Kim Guyer, who began to sense an accident that had happened at this mill many years ago. The male spirit appeared to come through as a young man and stated that he was injured badly at night in the building.

One of the investigators with NJPP, Marci Keck, was able to capture great spirit communication with the Phasmabox and her dowsing rods. The investigation can be seen on YouTube in its entirety. It was a very active location, to say the least, and I strongly encourage you to view it. What I want to go into detail and share with you here is about a location at Waterloo that affected me the most.

One of the old homes on the property we felt held a young girl's spirit. As the mediums began to read the location and Marci implemented the Phasmabox and dowsing rods, we began to receive answers to the story behind this location.

Home in Waterloo Village where we had the most activity.

In my mind's eye, I began to see images of a young girl running around the home and playing. When I receive images from spirits, they come across as an old movie playing in my mind's eye. I saw this young girl enjoying a beautiful day and just being a child. Through the investigation, we found out that she was very protected by her parents, almost kept in a bubble, and not allowed to play with the other town children. We even got a sense in death that the parental spirits were very protective of her.

I used my K2 Meter and seemed to have gotten into a spirit game of hide-and-seek with her. As I moved around the home, the meter would go off at certain locations. As I followed the K2 hits, I was led to the porch at the back of the home, where the K2 beeped one last time as the little girl spirit left.

Maryann Taylor, a medium who works with the Lady Ghostbusters, was close to me when this happened. She told me that the little girl spirit returned inside the home and was watching us from the upstairs window.

That connection with a child spirit deeply affected me. As a father of two small boys, I was moved to tears by the sad story of this playful little girl. Though her life was cut short due to illness, her spirit still shines on. When leaving that location, I told her I would come back and visit. I have kept my promise.

CHAPTER 6
NEW JERSEY
PARANORMAL PROJECT

IT WAS 2007 when I first had the idea to form New Jersey Paranormal Project, a team of paranormal investigators dedicated to the history of our state. I loved the paranormal shows on television and wanted to explore the historical locations in my area and showcase them to the public. We are truly blessed in this state to have so many historical connections to the land. Being one of the original thirteen colonies, New Jersey has seen history unfold in all of its counties.

History has always interested me, so I was naturally drawn to combining it with the paranormal and seeing if events that transpired so many years ago had an impact on the land and structures today. Above all, I wanted to know: Could intelligent or residual spirit energy from decades or centuries in the past still be felt and seen at these places?

NJPP Team at Waterloo Village (Left to right: Kyle, Kim, me, Hayden, Marci)

Prior to NJPP, my early investigations consisted only of a tape recorder and camera to capture photos at the locations. One of the most active areas where I always picked up something was Ringwood Manor, built on the site of a former ironworks in Passaic County.

Rich with Marci and Hayden Keck from NJPP

More than two hundred years ago, this country manor nestled in northern New Jersey was home to a succession of important ironmasters, including the Ryerson and Copper-Hewitt families—not to mention geographer and surveyor general of the Continental Army Robert Erskine.

It always felt to me that spirits were everywhere at this location. You could feel it as soon as you stepped on the property, almost like eyes were watching you from afar. It was not in a bad way or malicious; it was more out of curiosity than anything else.

On a visit to Ringwood Manor one summer after-noon, I was taking pictures of Sally's Pond and did not notice the image until I got back home. I must have taken over a dozen photos of the pond that day, but in one photo, you can clearly see what looks like a person floating on the surface of the pond.

Sally's Pond, Ringwood Manor

I often wondered if this could have been Sally making her presence known to me. It did not appear in any other photo I took that day and has always gener-ated so much interest among people I show it to. I continued to investigate the paranormal until about 2009, when, teaming up with a friend, I developed an outdoor video venture, *The Reel Deal Fishing Show*. We produced educational fishing videos as well as gave seminars and lectures all over the east coast.

While working on the fishing videos and writing articles for various outdoor magazines, I never gave up my love for the paranormal. I continued to watch paranormal programming and also enjoyed checking in with local paranormal research teams posting videos on YouTube.

New Jersey does have some very credible teams who share content through their social media platforms, and their videos are fantastic to watch.

Fast-forward to 2019… my wife and I had our first child, and my time out on the water was limited. I no longer could be away for those six- to eight-hour fishing trips. I was going through YouTube one day, and a recommended video popped up in my feed. The video was from a channel called Ghost History Medium. Not only were ghost and history, two of my favorite topics, both in the title, but the medium was investigating Hibernia Cemetery in Rockaway, New Jersey. This location was practically in my backyard and a place I always wanted to check out.

In a flash, that long-ago shelved project saw the light of day again. I sent an email to the Ghost History

Medium, and we agreed to meet up for a joint investigation of the Wildcat Ridge/Hibernia Mining location. It was a cold November afternoon when we arrived. There, I met Kim and her husband, Kyle, and immediately felt a connection. We chatted about possibly combining our efforts, and I mentioned my long-ago idea for NJPP.

The Hibernia Mine Bat Cave – Rockaway, New Jersey

Everything came together at the right time for NJPP: it really was like a greater force at hand that got us all together. In the coming months, I learned about a historical paranormal group being run at Picatinny Arsenal by Marci Keck with help of her son, Hayden, so I reached out and the rest is... history! The New Jersey Paranormal

Project was formed, and we have been going strong since.

It's so important to have all the working pieces in a group that help with all aspects of an investigation. It's very easy to get to a location and turn devices on and steamroll through the place. Being organized and having the information to back up your findings is vital to a proper investigation.

Having team members you can absolutely trust and who handle specific duties helps the research process and makes investigating locations so much easier. That describes NJPP. We're functioning on all cylinders, and we put together a comprehensive investigation.

I feel that intentions play a huge role in your success; if you don't have ulterior motives and you really want to educate the public and help tell these locations' stories, things will happen for you. Some doors that once were closed might seem to open if you're coming from a good place. Intentions are very important even when dealing with spirits.

I look forward to seeing what the future holds for NJPP and our team of experienced researchers. It has been a very long road to get where we are today, but it's been worth every mile.

CHAPTER 7
BUTLER MUSEUM

Butler Station, Butler, New Jersey

ON THE UPPER end of Main Street in Butler, New Jersey, sits the Butler Museum. The museum is a converted train station and contains items from the area's history. Some of the most notable pieces are from local schools and industries, like the American Rubber Company, as well as Thomas Edison and sculptor Frédéric-Auguste Bartholdi. That's only mentioning a few!

The Butler Museum is housed in an old train station, which was built in 1872 by the New Jersey Midland Railway, a predecessor of the New York, Susquehanna and Western Railway. This train station has seen history arrive at its doors and has such a story to tell. When NJPP reached out to Paul Bastante, who runs the museum and is the Butler historian, he invited us to come see the museum for ourselves. It's always a true pleasure investigating places like this, where the history and artifacts are on display and the information is readily at hand.

How NJPP works new locations typically starts with a pre-investigation visit. Through a pre-investigation, we want to make a connection with the contact person and a connection to the location. We also feel that it eases our group into the location and its spirits. At this stage, we not only collect information and answer questions from the contact person, but we also try to explain what we are doing in the location to the spirits. We don't want the spirits to feel that they just got bombarded by a group of people with devices that are demanding communication.

This kinder and gentler approach has always worked

in getting the unseen residents to cooperate. During a pre-investigation, we also take a ton of photos. This is to get an understanding of the layout of the space and let us share with group members who could not make the initial visit. In addition, it allows the possibility of catching anomalies or orbs. When I look at the photo-graphic evidence of past pre-investigations, I can't help but notice anomalies or orbs that show up. It's almost like spirits are checking us out from afar and observing us while at the location.

Orb captured next to marching band outfits.

When NJPP Investigator Marci Keck and I were in the museum's section that showcases the band uniforms, in one of the photos we took, you can clearly see an orb the size of a softball. It's a perfect circle and emitting a white light. Marci was also able to get some SLS mapping of a figure in one of the band uniforms. We knew at this point that this location was going to be very active and interesting.

Team Member from NJPP capturing SLS image of a figure.

Our investigation of the Butler Museum did not disappoint; it was active from the arrival of the NJPP team. Our medium, Kim Guyer, quickly picked up on a woman's presence on the outside platform. Kim went on to say that the woman was waiting for something to arrive, and it never did. She also picked up on different classes of people using the station, from workers to upscale weekend customers coming to the area. One of the most incredible images she saw was the coal coming into the station, which was validated by historian Paul Bastante as a routine delivery. It's always incredible when the history matches up to the mediumship reading of a location.

I was drawn to the center area of the museum, where the original ticket window is located. There, I immediately got an image in my mind's eye of a young boy from the early 1900s with a cap on his head running around the museum. I feel that when no one is around, he has the run of the place, and he likes it. So many items to play with, and it's his own train station!

Investigating the basement at the Butler Museum

I wanted to create the commotion of a train coming and possibly stir up activity—not to mention that Paul wanted NJPP to investigate during the morning rush at the station. While holding my K2 Meter near the ticket window, I began to state loudly, "Get your tickets! Leaving for New York!" It was at this moment that the K2 Meter started to get hits from spirit activity.

There is residual energy at the museum; it's like an old movie being played repeatedly. These images are attached to the very fiber of the historic building and to its artifacts on display. Then there's the intelligent spirit communication. In these cases, we ask spirits for a specific response—to make a device light up, move the dowsing rods, or use the Phasmabox and speak through this electronic tool—and we get one. These spirits have a message, and they want to communicate.

I think some spirits are not always at a location; they are energy and only a thought away. This idea is one that I have applied over the years to my understanding that possibly the spirit world works through talking with mediums.

Many experts say your deceased loved ones know you are thinking of them and can hear you talking to them. We can't know for sure how the spirit realm works, unfortunately, till we get there in spirit ourselves. So, this is my belief: when we visit museums and look at artifacts that meant so much to people who have crossed over from our would to the next, they can choose to open up communication with you. Their presence might take fondly to someone admiring their picture or achievements in life. I don't think these spirits are just sitting around the museum and waiting for the door to open. But if you come in with respect and kindness and are ready to listen, you might get a response.

In certain cases, however, I do believe that spirits can be attached to a location. They might have unfinished business there, or their life was cut short and they have an emotional attachment to the place. Some spirits have a strong message for the living or perhaps do not even know they are deceased. With such spirits, it can take some time to gain their trust and receive their message. They can be stubborn and not want to talk at all and choose to stay at the location.

In most cases, once the spirit gets their message across to the living, they feel that they can move on. It's often the case with people who claim that their home is haunted: once a medium comes into the location and gets the location's story, activity seems to slow down. All locations are not the same and neither are all spirits!

I strongly urge you to watch the Butler Museum episodes on the NJPP YouTube channel and come to your own conclusions. I would also highly recommend that you visit the museum and appreciate the history that awaits you inside.

CHAPTER 8
MY PURSUIT OF THE PARANORMAL

Investigating an old home in Boonton, New Jersey

MY PURSUIT of the paranormal has taken me down into many dark, dank basements and up into attics full of cobwebs that would give anyone the creeps. Places that ordinary people would not dare set foot in make a paranormal researcher get excited about the possibility of contacting spirits. Many a time, I have passed old cemeteries and abandoned buildings on my way to lighthearted family gatherings and thought to myself, "I need to remember this location to come back to and investigate."

Then there are the places that cross our paths by chance, places that we happen to stumble upon in our daily lives. It's almost like the universe is putting you where you need to be. Some people might even consider the synchronicities of things coming into place on our journey in this field. I strongly believe this; often, I have felt such a strong connection to people I met for the very first time when we collaborated on an investigation. There are always the people who come into our lives just at the right moment and help us with something we might not have been able to get through alone. There are no coincidences in this life: we are all spirits having a human experience.

When we let go of the human life, we once again join in the collectiveness of spirit. At this point, we can choose to move on and vibrate at a higher frequency, or we can choose to observe the living closely and remain on the earth realm.

I had the opportunity to have a reading with a medium who revealed that my grandfather, who passed way before I was born, chose to be one of my spirit guides. As she explained, my grandfather wanted to help me along my path.

The medium also told me that spirit guides might change over the course of our lives and move on when they feel their job is done. She described different guides that we can have in our lives here on earth, such as archangels, guardian angles, helper angels, spirit animals, ascended masters, and departed loved ones. To this day, I still receive signs from spirit and use them at times to make big choices in my life.

For me, one of the signs of a loved one who has crossed over is seeing a cardinal. A medium once told me that the cardinal is a symbol my grandmother uses to let me know she's around. When making up my mind on when to propose to the woman I had been dating, I asked my grandmother to show me a sign that it was the right time to pop the big question. We were driving home on Route 80, and a truck passed by us—what would you know, it had a cardinal football decal in its rear window. So I went home and proposed! The rest is history; I've been happily married for seven years.

When it comes to communicating with spirits, I suggest learning all you can from as many people as you can. In addition to reading books and watching videos, metaphysical festivals and spiritual churches offer so many programs to develop your spirit awareness and open yourself safely for contact.

St. Patrick's Cemetery, Rockaway Township, New Jersey

Many years ago, I participated in a séance at the Proprietary House in Perth Amboy, New Jersey. The Proprietary House was the governor's mansion of the original Thirteen Colonies and is still standing today. Overseen by architect and builder John Edward Pryor, construction began in 1762 and was completed in 1764. The séance was led by Jane Doherty, a highly respected psychic medium.

When in the circle, I definitely felt the air change and sensed a cool breeze moving around all of us who were joined by holding hands. As Jane spoke to and talked about the spirits of early American colonists who were present, I distinctly heard voices in my head, repeating, "Rations are low. The rations are low."

The séance was an incredible experience. Jane Doherty is truly a gifted psychic medium; it was a privilege to witness her firsthand. I later learned that the colonists did indeed have an issue with rations coming into the location during the Revolution, since its occupants were loyal to the Crown.

The pursuit of the paranormal is such a rewarding feeling when you can bring a voice to a location and contact its unseen inhabitants. At times, locations can be extremely quiet, and you spend more time talking to an empty room than a spirit. But then there are the times where the location comes alive, and all your tools help you tell their stories.

CHAPTER 9
SPIRIT IMAGES

Spirit sketch of the little girl from Waterloo Village

WHEN I INVESTIGATE LOCATIONS, I get images using my mind's eye, or what some refer to as your third eye. People who use this technique are tapping into their clairvoyance. Being clairvoyant is being able to see visions of the past, present, and future. These images flash through your mind's eye. They can seem to appear like a daydream. Sometimes, I am truly amazed by what I see when I visit locations.

Many years ago, when I was living in an apartment, my landlord learned about my interest in the paranormal and my developing abilities. He wanted to test me out on the location I was renting. He called me downstairs to the first floor of the home and had me walk through his floor. As soon as I entered the home, I got the image of an old woman looking out the front window. Her hair was up, and she was in a nightgown. I would have placed her in her seventies and described her as a grandparent.

I told him about the image I got and moved on down the hallway towards the bathroom and bedrooms. As I passed the bathroom, a white flashbulb went off in my mind's eye; I saw the same elderly woman lying on the bathroom floor, clearly in pain. When I told my landlord about this image, he abruptly told me to stop. I was not sure why he cut the reading short, but then he started to explain.

That apartment had belonged to his grandmother. She would watch him from the window and could always be seen peering out. Then he told me she had slipped and fallen in the bathroom and was hospitalized as a result of that accident. The sad part: she never got to come home from the hospital and passed without her family around her.

That was one of my first location walk-throughs, and I was quite proud of how I was able to connect with spirit. Now as I get older, I feel more comfortable with the connection, and it doesn't faze me. Sometimes, I still walk into locations and a flood of images—or just a single image—comes quickly. Not being a trained artist, I do my best in sketching the people I see. I try to recreate the spirit that is present in detail and as accurately as possible.

Sketch of little boy from Butler Train Station.

It's such a rewarding feeling when the client can confirm the images or the medium that I'm working with picks up on the same spirit. In the end, I believe that these spirits just want to be seen, heard, and acknowledged. They might have a message to convey, but often it's as simple as letting you know they are there.

If you want to develop your spirit imagery, I recommend this simple exercise:

1. Go to a place you haven't been before. I love going to historical places and learning about the locations that played an important role in history.
2. When you arrive, try to quiet your mind and focus on your third eye. Your third eye is located between the eyebrows; it is the center of intuition and foresight.
3. Close your eyes and open yourself to the location. You might well be surprised at how images start to play in your mind's eye.
4. Take the time to pay close attention to what you are seeing. It also helps to have a notepad close by or a tape recorder that you can use to document the experience.
5. If an image of a person appears, try your best to remember the details. I like to try to capture the following.

- What time period
- Physical attributes
- Person's age
- What are they doing?
- Clothing
- Symbols

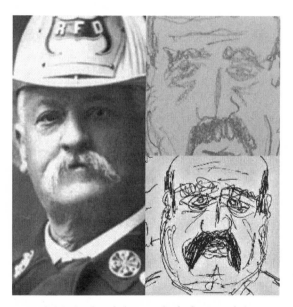

Spirit sketch and photograph of a fireman who's buried at Rockaway Township

Among the images you might get from historical places, you might see notable people you know going into them. If it's a home George Washington visited and you get an image of George, it can be argued that you know the subject. The funny thing at places like this, I get more images of the people who were behind the scenes. I'm talking about cooks, servants, family members, and guests.

Private homes let you focus on a blank slate—and going in not knowing anything and seeing what you come up with really tests your ability. The more you practice, the clearer things will start to become, and you will gain confidence in what you are receiving from spirit.

Along with practice, there are many meditation programs that help you develop these senses as well as lectures from outstanding people in the field. The Journey Within Spiritualists' Church, located in Pompton Lakes, New Jersey, is a great place to begin your search. This is a beautiful school and church run by fantastic people. They offer programs and classes to awaken your intuitive abilities.

CHAPTER 10
THERE ARE PLACES I REMEMBER

Photoshopped image of me, however, afterwards it looks like there's a Wendigo in the center.

BOONTON HISTORICAL SOCIETY and Museum

One of the locations NJPP investigated will probably stay with me for a long time. The Boonton Historical Society and Museum invited my team in for an investigation—and right from the start, this location was overflowing with spirit energy. The four-story-tall brick building was constructed in 1898 as a private residence for Dr. John Taylor and his wife, Adelaide Kanouse. It was used as office space for Dr. Taylor's medical practice, as well as the family residence. In 1901, Adelaide's ailing parents moved into the home. This arrangement was short-lived because her father died in 1905, and her mother died in 1908.

The history of the home is not entirely known, and finding the missing periods could make its story easier to tell. We do know that the Taylors faced a parent's worst nightmare: it is believed that they lost three children at the home. You can only imagine how traumatic those events could have been on the family. In his later years, what made Dr. Taylor move to Chula Vista, California, leaving the home and its tragedies behind him? His associate in the practice, a Dr. Peck, departed to serve in World War I and did not take over in Dr. Taylor's absence.

As our team proceeded to set up at the location and begin our walk through, we were taken down into the basement. As we descended the stairs, the ceiling lowered above our heads. We were met by that familiar musty smell of all things old. Though dimly lit, the basement was cleared of any belongings and easy to maneuver in. One section of the basement felt particularly active, so we focused our attention there.

In this area sat an old chair next to a window that

peered out onto the street, where life rushed by outside. You could not help but think of a spirit gazing out and seeing time unfold before their eyes. This would be the first location in the home we picked up and communicated with a spirit. We began to use the REM Pod, which allows spirit to manipulate and answer questions by approaching the device. The model I was using also detects temperature changes that spirits can cause in their attempt to communicate.

NJPP Team at the Boonton Museum

As I asked for responses, the REM Pod would activate and display lights and sound. I asked the spirit to make the device go off at the count of five, and it did exactly as I had requested. It would turn on and off on command, displaying an intelligence.

As we moved up to other floors, we continued to have great results with our tools and through our medium, Kim. This building has so many stories to tell and could benefit from countless investigations coming back to gather more of its paranormal history.

Backside of the Boonton Museum

The Boonton Museum's attic seems to be ground zero for the paranormal activity. Don't get me wrong—you could encounter spirits all through the building, but there was something about the stairwell that went up to the attic that really drew the team. On the last set of stairs going up into the attic, you could feel something trying to block you from entering. One of our team members, Marci, was gently pushed into the wall on the stairs. The attic felt much heavier than the rest of the home. It did not, however, feel like something malevolent in nature.

Entrance to Boonton Museum

This was one of the rare occasions that I was affected by the energy of the home physically. As I was investigating the attic, I felt a great sadness come over me, and my eyes started to well up with tears. I could not control the strong feeling I was experiencing and felt my heartbeat quicken, racing in my chest. I had to leave the home and step outside to let the feeling pass. It did go away after a few minutes of being outside and breathing in the cool winter air. Shortly after I returned and began walking up the stairs, the heaviness came back. I explained what had happened to my team and learned that they had all noticed the change that took place in me. I couldn't shake the feeling that the attic room was heavy with depression and sadness from an individual.

We were unable to determine if this was where the children had slept or perhaps where someone in the family went to be alone. The attic had previous reports of people entering from the stairs being pushed and not feeling welcomed. I feel that the spirit in the attic just wants to be left alone and, if addressed, to be approached with kindness and respect. This is definitely a location we will follow up on to peel back its layers and try to get more of its story. We will only find out what the spirits want us to know.

———

WHIPPANY BURYING YARD

The oldest cemetery in northwest New Jersey, the Whippany Burying Yard, dates back to 1718. Spanning just over two-plus acres, it has approximately 450 graves —including those of respected veterans of the French and Indian War, the American Revolution, the Civil War, and World War I. It is also the final resting place of many prominent Morris County public figures. The Whippany Burying Yard sits next to busy Route 10 and can be accessed from a parking lot next to it.

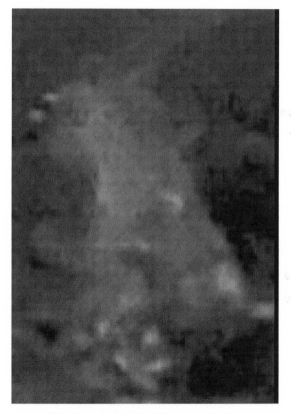

Mist I captured on film. Can you see the face forming?

When NJPP investigated this location, it was a late summer afternoon. Investigators Hayden, Marci, and I arrived as the sun started to set behind the trees next to the Whippany River. We began with a dowsing session and were guided towards the back-left corner of the burying yard. As Marci asked questions, the dowsing rods moved and answered yes or no. The dowsing rods are such a great old-school technique to implement in your investigations, especially when your locations are from a timeline in the 1700s, 1800s, or early 1900s. We feel that spirits might be more familiar with these old devices. According to some reports, the technique of dowsing goes all the way back to biblical times.

Whippany Burying Yard (Left to Right: Me, Marci and Hayden)

After the dowsing session, we turned on the Phasmabox and opened it up for spirits to speak through the digital device. The Phasmabox uses sound banks and internet radio stations to create an amazing verbal mix. With its advanced embedded reverb and echo features, it proves to be an amazing tool for our team time and time again. When you can ask a spirit a question and receive an intelligent response, it can chill you to the core.

During our investigation that evening, we got some really impressive responses from the Phasmabox. We also got the name Cory, and it so happens that the Cory gravestone was about fifty feet away from us.

At times I feel that when a device like the Phasmabox is turned on, many spirits jump at the chance to communicate. It's like setting up a microphone on a crowded dance floor—everyone wants to lean in and say something into it. Often spirits at the location are finally getting the opportunity to speak after so many years of silence. That's why I feel that we get so many voices when the Phasmabox is turned on. You will find that some voices will be stronger and more pronounced than others; it can be the case that they have more energy. I have heard some responses on the device that will immediately make you a firm believer in its ability to contact spirits.

The sun was gone from the sky, and darkness began to fall as Hayden, Marci, and I started to walk from the back of the burying yard towards the front. As we walked among the gravestones, you could not help but reflect on the importance these people played in our country's history, not to mention in our New Jersey history. The summer night gave us a few low-light glimpses of what we could see of the location. I took my cell phone out and started to take a burst of photos; I find low-light conditions are great for catching anomalies and orbs. Right before I began snapping away, I said out loud to any spirit who might be listening, "This is your last chance to make your presence known."

Shortly after, we ended the investigation and went our separate ways. It wasn't until the morning, when I started to go over the photographic evidence, that I noticed a white mist in the right corner of one of the photos I took. After playing with the photo and flipping it around, I could see a face staring back at me. You can clearly see human features, eyes and a nose, developing in the mist. This was captured in only one of the photos and could not be explained. I went back the next day to rule out webbing in the trees and found nothing to discredit the image.

I believe we were being watched as we investigated the location, and, in response to my invitation, a spirit wanted to make their presence known. When it came to evidence, as you can see in our YouTube episodes, it varied from dowsing to electronic devices. You can definitely feel spirits at the Whippany Burying Yard, and like all locations we investigate, if you respect them, the spirits won't mind the visit.

————

PRESBYTERIAN CHURCH OF ROCKAWAY, NJ

We were drawn to investigating the Presbyterian Church of Rockaway for its storied cemetery. Part of the present-day cemetery was believed to be an old Native American burial ground that dates to pre-colonial times. The colonial settlement took hold here around the year 1720. The founding of the church took place in 1758, with a sanctuary that was constructed in 1832. The cemetery is the final resting place for many people who have served our country since the Revolutionary War, including General William Winds, the only Revolutionary War general from Morris County, New Jersey.

It's said that some of the earliest settlers whose grave sites are unknown and forgotten could be under the large church parking lot or even under some of the cemetery roads. This is a beautifully kept cemetery, and so much work has gone into preserving the gravestones and its history. My team has collected some amazing evidence from this location, ranging from audio to photos. We were invited by the sexton of the church to investigate and agreed to let him know if we picked up on anything. From his years of serving as the sexton of the church and working on its grounds, including the cemetery, Rob has many stories of occurrences you can't easily explain.

Oldest grave marker in Rockaway Presbyterian Church Cemetery

Among his stories, Rob went on to tell us about a woman praying inside the church who encountered a little girl spirit watching her from a doorway. Based on the woman's description, the little girl looked to be ten years old or younger, and was just standing at the doorway, looking into the heart of the church. Then, as suddenly as she had appeared, the little girl vanished. The woman quickly exited the church and went on to see where the little girl had gone, and since she was so young, if an adult had come to get her. But no one was there. It truly was unexplainable.

Cemetery at Presbyterian Church in Rockaway, New Jersey

When this case was presented to NJPP, not only did I want to cover the cemetery, but I wanted to focus on the spirit of the little girl. I wanted to see if we could open the lines for communication and gain her trust. With younger spirits, I feel that using trigger objects they can identify with are key to getting reactions. Also, these objects can gain the spirit's trust and make them feel more comfortable with the individual investigating. In some cases with young spirits, we have noticed that older spirits protect them from coming through. When you think about it, it's so interesting to see spirits at locations looking out for and protecting one another. The one trigger object that I like to use for children is a Fisher-Price Laugh & Learn Smart Stages Puppy. This plush toy offers so many songs and colors that spirit can confirm and repeat back through our devices. The NJPP team has had great success and results with the Smart Stages Puppy, and it won't break your bank. You can typically buy this plush toy for less than fifteen dollars—it just might be the cheapest piece of paranormal equipment in your tool bag.

Motion sensor next to doll. Rockaway Presbyterian Church

On our return visit to the location, we placed the plush puppy in one of the pews in the front of the church. Our NJPP investigator Marci had her Phasmabox on, and as you'll hear in our YouTube episode, voices came through. When I pressed the plush puppy, it began to sing a song about colors. Once the song was over, I asked into the silence, "What did the puppy just say?"

The response that followed made the hair stand up on the back of my neck. You can clearly hear a child's voice say "red" and "purple." That was absolute proof to me that contact with a child had been made through the smart plush puppy.

Another helpful technique to use is simple: sing a few lyrics to a widely familiar children's song, like "Twinkle, Twinkle, Little Star," and see if you can get the young spirit you're communicating with to repeat it back to you. This also has worked when using devices that let you hear audible sounds. Knowing a few songs going back to the 1700s and 1800s can really help the spirits connect to you and get them to respond. Music can be a wonderfully effective way to bridge the gap in spirit communication.

THE LEGEND of Sleepy Hollow in Our Great Swamp

There is speculation that Washington Irving's "*The Legend of Sleepy Hollow*" might have its roots here in New Jersey. Irving was fascinated by George Washington—perhaps because he had the opportunity to meet the general in New York City when he was a boy. It was a lifelong pursuit of the author to one day write Washington's biography. It's highly possible that while Washington Irving was in Morristown doing research for his book on our founding father, he came across a legend that intrigued him. That legend was about a Hessian trooper who lost his head in the Great Swamp.

Sketch of the Headless Hessian of the Great Swamp. Sketch by Richard Moschella.

This could possibly be the origin of one of the most iconic characters in fiction and film: the headless horseman. The real Ichabod Crane was born in 1787 in Elizabethtown (now Elizabeth), New Jersey. From 1812 to 1857, he served in the United States Army. History shows that Washington Irving enlisted in the army in 1814 and served on the staff of Commander Crane in the New York State Militia. It's not a stretch to think that Irving learned about Commander Crane and might have tucked the name away in his memory for future use.

There is also a gravestone in the Presbyterian Cemetery in Morristown that bears an inscription on the back: "purchased by Ichabod Crane." There's also speculation that Irving could have seen that gravestone while visiting Morristown and later used the name in his book.

You can almost picture the scene of Washington Irving, while taking a break from his research, relaxing with the Morristown locals. I can imagine them asking, "Well, Mr. Irving, have you heard about the tale of the headless Hessian of the Great Swamp?" I believe the story Irving was told went something like this...

In the late 1770s, three Hessian soldiers were passing through Basking Ridge. At that time, the Great Swamp proved a difficult obstacle for horse-drawn travel. The swamp, however, provided a tactical advantage for the Continental Army to keep sight of the Redcoats, who, at times, tried to pass through it. One day, three Hessian soldiers were starting to make their way into the swamp when they were blindsided and attacked by local villagers. One poor Hessian almost had his head torn off his body by the angry mob. As the attack was happening, the mortally wounded Hessian's horse was spooked by the villagers and galloped into the darkness of the swamp. According to legend, the horse was spotted a few days later. Unfortunately, the presumably headless body of the Hessian rider was never found.

Here's how the locals might have ended their story: "So it's said, Mr. Irving, if you walk on the Great Swamp trails at night, you might hear a horse in the distance approaching you. You might even see the rider himself, and you know what he's doing. He's looking for his head."

You can't help but wonder if Washington Irving took what he learned about the headless Hessian of the Great Swamp back to Tarrytown, New York, and went on to write one of the greatest works of American fiction. Being a huge fan of the works of Washington Irving, I can't help but drive past the swamp and peer into the trees and try to catch a glimpse of the headless rider. Our New Jersey connection to the Headless Horseman of Sleepy Hollow is a story I would love to see the area embrace and welcome.

RINGWOOD MANOR

Ringwood Manor is in Passaic County, in northern New Jersey, and was the site of an ironworks and home to several well-known ironmasters. The area was also home to a geographer and surveyor general in the Continental Army, Robert Erskine. Erskine was a prolific mapmaker and drew more than 275 maps of the northern sector. Some are still used today by historians. He also kept Ringwood iron operating to supply the Continental war effort. Among Erskine's accomplishments, the iron from Ringwood produced the links for the chain that stretched across the Hudson River, a defensive device to stop British ships from getting close to West Point. The iron was also used by the army for many other purposes.

The current Ringwood Manor House was not built until 1807 and has since seen many families pass through its doors. In the early nineteenth century, Martin J. Ryerson purchased the historic ironworks and took over operations. Ryerson began building the impressive residence while still operating the iron mines and forges on the property. For the next half century, Ryerson ran five forge-furnace complexes in three counties from his headquarters at Ringwood. He made shot for the War of 1812 and helped the war efforts. Even at this point, Ringwood Manor had seen history happen from its doorsteps, not to mention notable figures who stopped at the estate on their way through New Jersey.

Ringwood Manor

Peter Cooper and his son-in-law, Abram S. Hewitt, purchased the property in 1854 and continued the iron-master duties at Ringwood. During the American Civil War, Cooper and Hewitt were major suppliers of the Union cause; they supplied gunmetal, among other items, for the Union Army pre- and post-Civil War Era.

The Hewitt family would later donate the home and land to the state of New Jersey in 1938. The property was declared a National Historic Landmark District in 1966. Over the years, many people who have visited the home, and some caretakers as well, have reported paranormal occurrences in Ringwood Manor.

Bizarre statue in statue garden at Ringwood Manor

Legendary paranormal investigator Hans Holzer visited the manor and devoted a part of his book *Ghosts of New England* to the spirit happenings there. As he shares, the medium he worked with channeled the spirit of a former servant at the manor, and the account that transpired is quite amazing and chilling. I highly recommend getting your hands on a copy of this book and reading the details of Holzer's investigation.

Ringwood Manor has drawn paranormal enthusiasts and teams to its location for years—everyone, it seems, is trying to capture something to validate the stories told of its haunted history. Unfortunately, at the time of this book's publication, Ringwood Manor no longer allows inside investigations due to incidents of vandalism and trespassing, in addition to Covid-19. It's such a shame that a place with so much history and spirit can't be investigated. We can only hope that, in time, this will change, and Ringwood Manor's paranormal history can be embraced along with its American history.

I have been going up to Ringwood Manor for years and love the dedication that the staff put into keeping this beautiful home as original as possible. The tours are always wonderful, and the Victorian Christmas events are stunning. You almost get the feeling that you have traveled back in time and are welcomed guests of the Hewitt family.

On my trips to Ringwood State Park and the manor, I

have always seemed to capture something of paranormal nature. On one occasion while walking by Sally's Pond, I captured the image of what appears to be a woman floating on top of the water. I wrote about that experience earlier in this book, and the photo still intrigues me to this day.

While on a visit there in the fall one year, I took another photo that turned out to be intriguing. It was a scenic shot, looking through the gates at the fall foliage and rolling hills. I printed it and gave it to my mother, who also loves Ringwood. I got a phone call from my mother a few days later, and she told me she saw a child in the photo. I pulled up the photo on my computer, looked at the area she pointed out, and asked her to repeat what she saw. My mom said, "It looks like a child's profile with a bonnet on its head in the tree line." After cropping the photo and enlarging it, I could see what she was talking about.

In 2020, the NJPP team went to Ringwood Manor to do an investigation on the grounds and captured some interesting evidence. We conducted a Phasmabox session and feel that Robert Erskine communicated through the device. We got some very clear responses that would point towards the spirit being that of Erskine. We also used the dowsing rods and asked the spirits if they remembered Hans Holzer visiting the home. They responded with a yes.

Profile picture of an apparition of a little boy on the treeline.

The team was astonished that the spirits haven't forgotten Holzer. It also showed us that spirits can remember and retain memory from years past. They can recall people who visited the home and communicated with them. That's why it's so important to conduct yourself in a professional manner while investigating locations and dealing with the living and the dead.

In the YouTube episodes, you will see that we do our best to cover the entire grounds of Ringwood Manor and conclude our investigation at the cemetery. As the team all felt, once we got to the cemetery's gravel road, the energy changes—the best way to describe it is a fluttering or tingly feeling. I experience it on my shoulders first when I encounter spirits. It almost feels like a light electric current that comes over you. Then it's usually followed by the feeling of having someone standing behind you and being watched. The NJPP team all confirmed the feeling in this area at the same time of entering it. This is a place so full of spirits, and from what we gathered, these spirits are more than willing to tell their stories. We experimented with dowsing rods and the Phasmabox, and both worked extremely well in the cemetery.

SAINT PATRICK'S Cemetery

Located in the Hibernia section of Rockaway Township, nestled in the forest of Wildcat Ridge, lies Saint Patrick's Cemetery, also known as Hibernia Cemetery. Only about forty headstones have survived of the 440 souls who are laid to rest here. I discovered its whereabouts when I moved to Rockaway Township back in 2014. I heard this cemetery mentioned a few times in conversation with the locals, and it got my attention. With a quick Google search, I found that it appeared on a map in the middle of the woods in Wildcat Ridge wildlife management area. This location was literally in my backyard and only about a ten-minute drive from my house. What's more, it appeared to be off a hiking trail and easy to access. I watched a few videos on YouTube to get the layout of the trail and pinpoint where the cemetery was. It's always good to get an idea of the terrain and notice any major parts of the trail when going into a place like this.

Headstone in St. Patrick's Cemetery

When the day came, I arrived at Wildcat Ridge and began my hike into the cemetery. I noticed a small skeleton that someone hung in a tree as I got near to the entrance. Then I noticed some faded silk flowers that looked like they might have been there for some time. Then I noticed the stones through the trees.

As I entered the cemetery, I could not help but think to myself, "This looks like something right out of a Stephen King novel." It even had the old wooden sign with letters weathered and faded; some are even missing. The place really gives you all the feels. As you enter it, you notice how quiet everything seems to get. It's almost as if the forest is paying its respects to these souls.

NJPP and the Lady Ghostbusters

Established in 1869, this location sits between upper and lower Hibernia and was a major area for mining.

Mining in this area goes back to the mid-eighteenth century, and you will still see some of the old remnants of mining in the surrounding woods. At some of the old structures, we have gotten hits on our K2 Meters. This device is very popular among paranormal investigators because it measures the electromagnetic fields at the location. The changes in the electromagnetic field will trigger lights to go off on the device and can signal spirit communication.

St. Patrick's Cemetery in Rockaway, New Jersey

For instance, if you were to ask the spirit to use the K2 Meter to respond to your questions by lighting up the device, and the lights go on and off accordingly, that can be compelling evidence for communication. I have asked spirits to light the device to a certain color on the meter and have gotten a direct response. Since we believe that spirits are energy, this is a great tool to have and document their presence at a location.

In the cemetery on another investigation, I took along a trigger object. I found out through research that the miners in the area would partake in drinking and everything that comes with overindulging in spirits of the drinking kind. I made sure to bring an old bottle of whiskey with me and wanted to see if that would trigger a response. Our investigator Marci Keck was using the Phasmabox, and voices could be heard coming through the speaker. As I took the bottle out of my backpack, I asked out loud, "What am I holding?" We immediately heard a voice say very loud back, "Vodka."

Unfortunately, whiskey was not the drink of choice for this particular spirit. I made a note to self to bring back a bottle of vodka next time.

Towards the end of the investigation, I opened up the bottle of whiskey and poured it out on the ground outside the cemetery. As the aged whiskey hit the cold dirt, another voice came through the Phasmabox—again, everyone heard it so clearly. You can hear a voice in the video say, "Sip, sip, sip." The spirit was probably wondering why I was wasting the whiskey and letting it pour until the bottle was empty. The whiskey quickly was absorbed by the dirt, and the evidence was captured. The experiment was a success: there definitely was a connection with spirits.

Bottle of whiskey being using a trigger object. REM pod positioned next to it to pick up on electrical magnetic fields.

The investigations at Saint Patrick's Cemetery can all be seen on the NJPP YouTube channel.

CHAPTER 11
ENCOUNTERS WITH SPIRITS

Sketch I did of my son seeing an apparition.

I WANTED to publish a book to take the reader along on our journeys filming the New Jersey Paranormal Project. I also wanted to create a publication that can help as a guide to understanding the paranormal world that is always around us. We live in a world that is full of spirits, and if we just slow down and listen, they want to communicate. Through my encounters, I want you, the reader, to understand what has fueled my passion and research in the paranormal.

During the writing of this book, my oldest son, who is about to turn two, started to show signs of sensitivity to spirit. My wife and I began to notice him looking into parts of the house and seeing something we did not. We have a digital picture frame connected to our files of photos. One night, a photo of my wife's grandfather, who passed away long before our son was born, appeared. It was a black-and-white photo of when he was in the service in World War II. Our son was watching a show on the television and turned his head to see the photo. Without hesitation, he said, "Ghost." Halloween had just ended and since he'd been saying, "ghost" often around the house, we did not think much of it.

Weeks went by, and we're in December, getting the house ready for Christmas. Suddenly, our son had a very scared look on his face. He backed up and hid behind one of his toys, and we heard him saying, "Pa, Pa, Pa." My wife was starting to get freaked out by not being able to see what he was seeing. Also, why was it frightening him so much seeing "Pa"? After a very brief period, he went back to playing with his toys. My wife just gave me the look, as if saying, "What did you bring home from your readings?"

That night as I went to bed, I started to wonder, who could that, "Pa" be? I was thinking about our family members who had passed on, and going through names and nicknames, when one hit me like a ton of bricks. My grandfather had passed away back in 2009 and never met our children. Our youngest's middle name is Dominick after him. I hardly ever called him grandpa. Since I was a child, I would always call him Pop. I had been sitting with Pop when he crossed over into spirit after suffering a long battle with mesothelioma. When the time came, he motioned for the window to his room to be opened, gave a wave to those of us who were gathered outside, and was gone.

If this was the "Pa" whom our son was seeing, I was almost brought to tears that Pop was checking in on him. The next morning, I pulled up a black-and-white image I had of Pop on my phone and asked our son if he knew who this person is. He looked at the photo, and his first words were, "Pa, Pa, Pa." He was scared all over again, so I put my phone down and let some time go by. I pulled up some photos that were in black and white of other men to see if he called them "Pa." I just wanted to rule that possibility out and be certain that this "Pa" was Pop. I showed him a black-and-white photo of Elvis Presley and a few pictures of older men from random Google searches. He was pretty unfazed, and he called no one "Pa." After that, my wife was certain that our grandfathers were checking in on us.

She was concerned, however, about how it was scaring our son by his reaction to seeing them. I explained to her that, unfortunately, all sensitives have this to deal with as children. They have not learned how to turn themselves off yet to the ability. In all the books I have read on mediums who talk about early childhood experiences, this is the time that is most uncomfortable to deal with.

I did my best to explain to my very young son that it was okay to see his two great-grandpas, and that they are watching out for him. It's okay if they might look different from us or you might see through them. If you ever feel scared, you can tell them to go away, and they will listen. If you want to use your special powers, picture a very bright white light all around you and ask them to leave.

As I know from trying with my two-year-old, it's hard to teach grounding and the techniques to handle intuitive abilities to a young child, but you can try to simplify some basic ideas of protection. Start by reassuring the child that it is okay to see what they are experiencing. I believe children can see into the spirit world and are more connected to the other side. This can also explain why some children have imaginary friends that they play with, or why some children stare off into nothingness and say they are talking to someone you can't seem to see.

When children with sensitivities start school, they begin to work with the left side of the brain and shut off their creative right side of the brain. As a result, the gift of intuition becomes duller and duller and then nonexistent. The left side of the brain is more analytical; subjects like math and science are what make sense. We start to see things in black and white and forget about the gray areas. Sensitivity to spirit is like every other skill you develop: if you don't work at it, it will eventually go away.

I can still remember encounters I had with spirit as a child and told no one about. One memory that is still vivid is seeing a spirit, a man, in my room when I was playing with toys. The man told me to get my mom, so I raced into the kitchen to let her know about the man in my room. When we went back to the room, the man was gone, and there was just a pile of my toys on the floor. As I grew up, I let go of this sensitivity and let the left-brain way of thinking take over. There would still be times that I would get the sense of someone who had passed before the news came or an idea of something happening before it did. If I did sense something, I spoke nothing about it and kept any visions of spirit people to myself.

As I became an adult and a paranormal researcher, I

learned to embrace these abilities and continue to develop them. Through the work of NJPP, I have been given the greatest classroom with some of the best teachers in spirit communication and paranormal research. I have learned so much from the people I met on this journey and hopefully helped others along the way. It's all about growing and continuing your education in the field. With matters of spirit, nobody knows everything.

———

HELLO, John, It's Dad

I was talking with a friend one day, and the topic of conversation turned to the paranormal and my research. John is a middle-of-the-road kind of believer with mix of skepticism about things he can't explain. He began to tell me the story about when his dad passed away and an event that would leave him stunned.

After a long, painful battle, the inevitable day came when his father lost his fight to cancer. As John returned home to prepare to make the necessary arrangements, his phone began to ring. He just couldn't manage to get up and listen to another phone call from another person sending him their condolences and telling him how great a man his father had been. He already knew that firsthand, and the emotions of never being able to hear his father's voice again left him in absolute grief.

As John sat on the couch, remembering the last time he saw and spoke to his father, the ringing from the phone stopped and the answering machine picked up. As he sank into the couch, the voice on the answering machine made him freeze in shock—it was the voice of his recently deceased father. His father's voice said, "Hello, John, it's Dad."

When the brief call ended, John sat there in disbelief. This was a routine he and his father had every weekend. When his father pulled up in front of his house, he would always call and let John know he was outside waiting.

John went to the answering machine and pressed play, thinking to himself that he had probably imagined what he'd heard. He was certain that the caller who left the message was not going to be his dad. He took a breath, and then his father's voice said, "Hello, John, it's Dad."

John then thought of the possibility that maybe, just maybe, the call was late coming through the cell phone service that his father had. He told himself that it was something along those lines—dead people don't leave messages on answering machines.

John played the message for his mother and other members of his immediate family, and they all were brought to tears. His loved ones felt that it was his dad's spirit letting them know he was okay and still with them.

John really wishes he'd picked up the phone that day and thinks about the conversation he could have had with his father. I told him that it was all meant to be the way it happened. By letting the call go to the answering machine, John was able to share the message with those close to his father and offer proof of spirit communication.

CHAPTER 12
THE NJPP TEAM & TOOLS WE USE FOR SPIRIT COMMUNICATION

NJPP Investigators Hayden and Marci Keck at the Butler Museum presenting a seminar for NJPP on the tools we use for investigations

IT'S SO important to surround yourself with people who complement your researching techniques. When putting NJPP together, I wanted to try my best to surround myself with a well-rounded team to investigate the paranormal with. I wanted to combine old intuitive techniques and modern electronic gear that is showcased on some of the leading paranormal television shows. Putting all the gear aside, it was important to find the right people to fit the group.

For NJPP, everything thing seemed to fall into place, and the team was formed. It's true what they say about intention: if it's coming from the right place, it will happen if you don't give up on it. We really want to tell the stories of spirits and the locations; I feel, "ghost hunt" is not the right phrase for what we do at NJPP. I prefer to call it a conversation with spirits. If they don't feel like communicating, that's fine with us too.

———

MEDIUMSHIP:

Mediumship was one of the tools I wanted to bring into the group; the medium would be a conduit to the spirit at the location we would investigate. A highly trained medium can really help a location open up and make contact with spirits who are willing to communicate. The gift of mediumship and psychic ability is astonishing to watch in action when we arrive at the locations and the stories begin to take shape.

- Clairvoyance: Clear Seeing: Clairvoyance is when images of the past, present, and future flash through our mind's eye much like a daydream. Your mind's eye is also known as your third eye and sixth chakra. Located on your forehead between your eyebrows, it is the center for intuition and foresight. Clairvoyance is one of my strongest abilities. When I arrive at locations, I begin to see images like an old movie being played out in my mind's eye. Some of the images are so clear to me, and I can't help but sketch them when I return home from investigations.

- Clairaudience: Clear Hearing: Clairaudience is hearing sounds or music in your mind that are being communicated by spirits. Spirits may be able to create audible sounds and music to convey a message—though this takes a tremendous amount of energy.

- Clairsentience: Clear Feeling: Clairsentience is feeling spirit emotions and physical pain at an investigation; it's also having a gut feeling. I worked with a few mediums who have picked up on ailments and emotions of the deceased. In addition to clear seeing, I have been affected with clear feeling. For example, while walking up into the attic during our investigation of the Boonton Museum, I was overcome with grief and sadness. I had tears welling up in my eyes and had to step outside the location to let the feeling pass.

- Clairalience: Clear Smelling: Clairalience is being able to smell odors or fragrances that don't have any kind of physical source, such as detecting the faint smell of flowers in a dark, closed room. Some might pick up a loved one's signature fragrance, the perfume or cologne they used in life, or the smell of their grandfather's workshop. When visiting the Mark Twain house in Hartford, Connecticut, a tour guide mentioned in his study some people say they smell his cigar smoke.
- Clairgustance: Clear Tasting: Clairgustance is the ability to taste something without the physical act of eating or drinking. Some might taste the holiday cookies or cake a loved one baked or the coffee they routinely drank.
- Claircognizance: Clear Knowing: A sense of claircognizance occurs when spirit communicates truths that simply pop into our minds like events in life that will happen. This could be something you've been hoping for,

like a marriage proposal or a promotion at work, or a challenge ahead you need to prepare for.

———

EQUIPMENT:

- Dowsing Rods

Conducting a dowsing rod session

Dowsing is a type of divination that was first used in practical attempts to locate groundwater or buried metals. As an occultist technique, dowsing is believed to have originated in Germany during the sixteenth century and was practiced by Martin Luther. There is other evidence, however, that dowsing dates back to ancient Egypt and may be depicted in hieroglyphics.

The dowsing response is generally attributed to the ideomotor response: a psychological phenomenon that occurs when the person holding the dowsing rods makes them move unconsciously. With dowsing rods, you can typically receive yes and no answers from a spirit. For me, when the rods cross, that means yes, and when the open widely, that is a no. When the rods remain open and pointing out, to me that is an unsure response. You will find that dowsing rods can be an effective tool to use and implement in your investigations.

- <u>Phasmabox</u>

K2 Meter and Phasmabox

The Phasmabox is a great technical tool that we use in connecting with spirits. It's a clear and responsive way to receive messages. It was released from Extreme Senses Software in 2015 and has since been featured in many paranormal television shows. This software mainly uses sound banks, but also uses internet radio stations to create an amazing mix. It offers a reverse mode that can be extremely helpful to implement during an investigation.

I have heard such clear and intelligent responses come from the Phasmabox. If you watch any episode of the New Jersey Paranormal Project, you will be able to see it being used and hear the proof of how the box helps the team tell the location's story. I am frequently amazed by how Phasmabox messages match up to the impressions we are getting through mediumship.

- K2 Meter

K2 Meter – REM Pod – Phasmabox

A popular tool for paranormal researchers, and one that's very affordable and very easy to use, is the K2 Meter. It detects spikes in the electromagnetic energy. When the K2 Meter encounters a spike, multicolor lights at the top of the meter signify spirit activity.

- Spirit Radio

The SBox Ghost Scanner radio frequency sweep scanner in action at a restaurant investigation

A spirit radio lets you use FM or AM band sweeps for spirit communication. The radios let you control the speed of the sweep and also have forward and reverse modes. Some of these devices will pause on a frequency when a voice comes through, allowing the message to be communicated. I have been using the SBox Ghost Box in investigations and find it very useful. I prefer using the AM sweep and have heard very clear voices come through.

During our investigation of a home in North Jersey, the SBox had a voice come through that said, "German." The home was close to a site known for its Hessian presence during the Revolutionary War. At another location, we were investigating the basement when a voice on the radio clearly said, "Psychic." At that time, a psychic medium was in the upstairs of the home. Spirit radios work. If spirits are energy, it makes sense that radio frequencies would be a great way to connect.

- Ovilus

S-Box Spirit Radio and Ovilus

Part of our investigation arsenal, the Ovilus is another tool that helps build the location's story. This device offers direct communication with spirits by converting the phonetic responses from environmental readings into words. Spirits may be able to alter the electromagnet frequencies in an environment, and the Ovilus takes advantage of this by leveraging these frequencies to choose a response from a preset database of over two thousand words.

At times, we get very interesting responses at locations that help during our investigation. In one location we investigated, there had been a very bad fire, and lives were lost. Picking up on the spirit's sounds, the Ovilus's screen lit up with the words Fire, Burn, Gone, and Death.

- REM Pod

REM Pod

The REM Pod uses a mini telescopic antenna to radiate its own independent magnetic field around the instrument. This electromagnetic field can easily be influenced by materials and objects that conduct electricity.

The new 2.0 version has ambient temperature deviation detection and raises the bar on how effective this device is for paranormal research. Having the REM Pod at locations really helps us detect intelligent responses from spirit and gives us a physical idea where a spirit is in the room. One result that always amazes me: when you ask a spirit to step towards or touch the device, it goes off; then when you ask a spirit to back away, the device goes silent.

- Trigger Objects

Combining a trigger object and the REM Pod

A trigger object could be several things, or just about anything, that will get the spirit you're communicating with to respond. This can range from a tool that the spirit might have used in life to colors, symbols, or even singing a song. In some locations, holding up an object and asking out loud, "What am I holding?" or "What color is this?" may be enough to trigger a response. In locations with children's spirits, toys, especially ones that light up and play music, often work wonders as trigger objects.

- Pendulum

Using a pendulum for communication with a spirit

A pendulum works by tapping into your intuition and sixth sense. The pendulum acts as a form of receiver and transmitter from your higher guidance, guardian angels, and spiritual teachers. As the pendulum moves, you gain answers in response to questions. Like dowsing rods, it is best suited to questions with simple yes or no answers. (For me, when the pendulum swings left to right, that means no. When it swings in a circle, that means yes.) Some people describe the way a pendulum works as bringing together your rational and intuitive sides, or the left and right sides of your brain. When these two elements are brought together, you're able to make decisions using all of your resources.

———

IT'S important to remember that these items are all part of our investigation toolbox. We are always learning about new devices and developments in our field. These tools work together in building a location's story and message from spirits. But the most important part and tool in an investigation is you: the person who is operating the devices and interpreting the messages. It's crucial not to rush an investigation and to try to disprove your findings. Before you label something as paranormal or a message from a spirit, you want to be sure you did your best investigating and presenting the evidence to your client. Some clients right from the start want something to be paranormal and at times can easily be discredited.

There was a location my team visited where the clients went out and bought a K2 Meter and started to film their own videos in the home, documenting the activity. When the NJPP team arrived, we noticed a large cell phone tower on the next street over from the home. The high electromagnetic field readings were due to this tower being so close to the home. The house did have spirit activity, but we had to implement different devices to uncover its story.

NJPP Investigator Marci Keck with EMF Meter

My advice: when going into a location, do your research and gather as much information as you possibly can beforehand. I create binders with information from historical sources and death records; this helps when we use certain devices to trigger responses from spirits. It is a great way to validate the responses you get.

When I leave a location, I like to ground myself when I return home. When you're dealing with different energies, it's important to cleanse your intuitive self. Here are some easy ways to ground yourself that only take a few minutes.

Connect with the earth. Take a walk in nature and breathe in the fresh air all around you. Try to cast out any mental chatter that creeps in, focus on your breath, and count the steps you are taking. Get your hands dirty and touch the earth. If water is present, touch that too. Lean on a tree and feel the bark's texture on the palm of your hand. Nature has many healing abilities, and it's all around us.

Some mediums I have worked with say that gardening is an excellent way to ground yourself.

Taking a bath with natural healing salts and water is a winning combo for its cleansing properties.

Here is a visualization technique that also is a great way to ground yourself. Imagine your feet are roots. With every breath you take, you extend your roots deeper into the ground under you. You are anchoring yourself deep into the earth. Take deep breaths and allow your energy to balance itself.

I hope this section will help you in building a team or just researching the paranormal yourself. It's very important to be serious and not to take this field lightly. When going into any location, make sure you show respect and kindness for spirits.

CHAPTER 13
HISTORICAL INVESTIGATIONS

IT'S ALWAYS a pleasure when we encounter people who have seen our work and found us on the internet. This is a wonderful community of good people who share a passion for investigating and bringing credibility to this field. The question always comes up: Where should I go to have a paranormal encounter or to communicate with spirits? I like to explain that, since spirits are all around us, you can try to communicate just about anywhere. My advice: do not start in your home in case you don't want to know who's living with you. My wife told me she does not want to know if I pick up on anyone in our home, so I keep that information to myself.

I would recommend going to historical parks or battlefields that are open to the public. It is also important to go during regular park hours—do not trespass.

These historical places need to be respected, and laws need to be obeyed by investigators. There's a widely held misconception that paranormal researchers trespass into locations at night. It is not true at all, but has brought a stigma to our field. Hopefully through respectful research, we can gain the trust of some of these historical parks and grounds.

NJPP investigates cases at all times of day—if spirits are at a location, they are there during the day as well as at night. When we investigated a train station, we found that the morning was a busy time for the spirit activity to pick up, which makes sense if you think that in life people came into this station to catch trains for work and return home. The peak rush-hour times are still active for spirits.

The following is a list of historical locations that I have been to and picked up on spirit activity. Some were also featured on paranormal television shows and visited by legendary paranormal investigators. These places also contain a wealth of information on New Jersey's history. Some of them are places where our history was forged, and its foundations can still be touched. Go with respect and an open mind for your conversation with spirits.

———

LAMBERT CASTLE

Paterson, New Jersey

Lambert Castle, Paterson, New Jersey

The castle was built in 1892 by silk tycoon Catholina Lambert. When it was built, it was known as Belle Vista. Lambert's dream was to build a home that captured the castles he remembered from his childhood in Great Britain. The castle has seen many notable visitors, including President William McKinley and Vice President Garret Hobart in 1898.

The Lamberts had eight children together, but only two lived to adulthood. The 1870s and 1880s were filled with both the joy of birth and the sorrow of death. This location has seen history made all around it and the city of Paterson become the busy city it is today. It has been said that the Lamberts' spirits are still very active at this location, and the castle has been featured on the Travel Channel's *The Holzer Files*.

THE WHIPPANY BURYING Yard
Hanover, New Jersey

Established in 1718, the Whippany Burying Yard is the oldest cemetery in Morris County. The two-acre burying yard has 450 gravestones. Among those buried are eleven Revolutionary War soldiers, several Civil War soldiers, and a few veterans of the French and Indian War, along with members of important local families who lived around Whippany, the first established village in Morris County.

One of the first settlers buried here is linked back to Emperor Charlemagne and forward to both Presidents Bush. This also is the final resting place of Colonel Joseph Tuttle, commander of the Morris County Militia, and Abraham Kitchel, an early settler, both of whom became original Morris County judges. This location was featured on an NJPP segment, and as discussed in an early chapter, we were able to collect a lot of evidence from the burying yard.

MORRISTOWN, New Jersey

Jockey Hollow Cemetery

NJPP Investigating Jockey Hollow in Morristown, New Jersey

One town in New Jersey I find myself continually investigating is Morristown. It seems like no matter where you go in Morristown, there are reminders everywhere of its importance in history. It has been called "the military capital of the American Revolution" because of its strategic role in the war for independence from Great Britain. The winter of 1779 to June 1780 found the Continental Army encamped at Jockey Hollow; it would become known as the worst winter of the Revolutionary War. The army faced lack of pay, scarce resources, and starvation. The entire Pennsylvania contingent successfully mutinied, and more soldiers tried to follow in their footsteps unsuccessfully. Many of the soldiers' health was weakened, and many perished during the frozen New Jersey winter.

It was at Morristown that the Marquis de Lafayette came to General George Washington with the news that France would send ships and experienced soldiers to help the American cause. This would be a pivotal move and start to change the tide in the American fight for independence.

The Wick House in Jockey Hollow

Benedict Arnold's court-martial hearing was held in Morristown, at Dickerson Tavern on Spring Street. Alexander Hamilton courted and married Elizabeth Schuyler in Morristown, at a home where Washington's personal doctor lived. The town has so much rich history, and places with rich history are always interesting locations to investigate.

Locations like Morristown have residual and intelligent spirit energy. Through NJPP, we have documented both in our case files. Also, there's the anguish of the harshest winter the Continental Army faced with all the death and despair. These imprints are still on the land at many of its locations, and some of these spirits are still here among us. They might have chosen to remain in a place they were so connected to in life, or they might still have unfinished business left on the earth plane. In some locations, I feel they might just want their story to be told and to be acknowledged.

———

JONATHAN'S WOODS

Denville, New Jersey

Nestled in the mountains of Denville and Rockaway New Jersey, Jonathan's Woods is so rich in history. The Hog Pen was used by settlers who, after learning about the events that transpired in northwestern New Jersey not too far from the area, were afraid of hostile Native Americans. The Hunt-Swartwout Raid was a horrific massacre that occurred in 1756. The colonial settlers who were living in the Swartswood area were totally unaware of the events that were about to unfold. The upper valley of the Delaware River and the northwestern corner of the state was sparsely populated wilderness frontier land. It is said that about five Lenape Indians crossed the Delaware River into New Jersey and proceeded on foot to the homes of three militia officers: Richard Hunt, Anthony Swartwout, and Daniel Harker. The Lenape destroyed the settlement, burying all the homes and killing Swartwout and several members of his family. At the end of the raid, members of the Hunt and Swartwout families were taken and held captive for several years.

Once this report made it down into the towns surrounding Denville, the settlers in the area knew they needed to come up with a plan. The Hog Pen would offer a place of protection in the dreaded event of a similar invasion. Fortunately, a hostile attack did not happen in the area, but the settlers would not forget the benefits of the Hog Pen's protection. During the American Revolution, area settlers and farmers would stash their livestock, food, and any valuables in the Hog Pen to keep them out of the hands of British troops.

Ghost History medium Kim and Rich at the Hog Pen in Denville, New Jersey

The woods here have a presence to them, which, as you walk their trails and especially into the Hog Pen, you can pick up on if you're a sensitive or intuitive. Once you descend into the Hog Pen, you can almost see the history playing out in front of your eyes. The mountain creates protection on every side, and you can feel how protected the settlers in the area felt here.

"The name Jonathan's Woods comes from the last known Native American to live in the area," confirms Vito Bianco from the Denville Historical Society. "There's an actual grave on the property," he notes to strengthen his point. "Unmarked," he adds, "and known only to a few." Legend has it that Jonathan and his wife lived out their years in seclusion on the hill, rarely venturing from their perch.

When I researched the location with the NJPP team, we got intelligent responses on the K2 Meter that followed us around the area of the Hog Pen. When I asked the spirit we were communicating with to light the K2 Meter to yellow, it did just that and then to red. It's always such a rewarding experience to get such clear responses. To my mind, when you ask for a specific reaction and receive that from a spirit, it confirms an intelligence over residual.

During our investigation, we also picked up on the name "David" as the individual who was communicating with us. Picking up on images, I saw David as an older man with a hat and stubbly beard. He had a love for the area and telling its story. He was also very protective of it and kept following the team as we investigated.

———

I PERSONALLY LOVE INVESTIGATING historical places. Besides researching the paranormal, I'm an avid reader of history and love to attend living history events. It's this love that also fuels my investigations—not only do I want to collect evidence, but I also want to find out who the spirit is and the story they are trying to convey.

The research process after an NJPP investigation is very interesting and critical to have responses match up to historical fact. In some cases, our investigations have even filled in the gaps in unrecorded history at locations. If what we find fills in missing accounts in a historical record, we ask the client to make note and share that this was communicated through spirit.

I am not trying to alter the history of any location or upset historians. However, if NJPP can provide some information to help fill in the missing pieces of an historical record or validate an event or person's experience, then we've provided a valuable service. That's our mission! We respect history and all the people who have come before us. One day, someone will be telling our story. We will be watching, possibly in spirit, hoping they get it right.

CHAPTER 14
THE END
(AND THE BEGINNING)

At the Old Dutch Church, Tarrytown, New York

IT'S VERY true that the end is just the beginning of something new. Everything we face in life has an end to it. If you think about it, your life has been full of ends, but at those ends were new beginnings. I like to think that is how the afterlife works: when we leave the body behind and go into spirit, it's the beginning all over again for us. We will simply shed the weight of the human existence and move into the realm of spirit. Death is not something to be afraid of, as I have heard many people who communicate with spirits say, and have come to believe myself.

It's all just a transition from this world to the next. Investigating and having my own personal experiences, I know deep down in my being that we do go on and this is not all there is. I feel that our time on earth is almost that of a classroom. We get to have human experiences. We learn about love and loss and the trials and tribulations that go with living a life. As me move into spirit, we bring those lessons with us. Those we communicate with in spirit from here on earth have messages they want to get across. They want to tell their stories and let the living know they are still here.

Some encounters with spirit have helped the living avoid tragedy or informed them of a tragedy to come. I have talked to so many clients who have lost loved ones close to them and have felt their loved one's presence comforting them in times of need. Spirit is all around us; our loved ones are only a thought away. To this day, I still have conversations with those I've lost, especially my grandparents. I can tell you for sure: I receive signs back.

I first conceived the idea of starting my own paranormal research team back in 2007. I filmed a few test videos with the New Jersey Paranormal Project as the title and then got involved with a very busy venture in professional fishing. I got to travel, present seminars on fishing, and work with professional anglers. I also gained valuable experience writing for outdoor magazines and contributing articles to fishing companies. Then, with the birth of my first son, life slowed down.

I had time to look at that shelf we all have—that shelf in your mind with all those unfinished projects sitting on it. When I looked at the shelf, I saw the New Jersey Paranormal Project and felt it was time to dust it off and make it a reality. Then everything came into place, and it happened.

The end of something became a new beginning. A chance to explore incredible locations and work with so many talented individuals in the field of spirit communication and the paranormal. It has been a true pleasure working with clients and learning about their locations and the spirits who reside there. In the locations we investigate, spirits are definitely present. We hope to continue telling their stories.

This is my paranormal project.

CHAPTER 15
A PLACE SPIRITS CALL HOME

Client's home in Morris Plains, New Jersey

AFTER THE PUBLISHING of my first book, *My New Jersey Paranormal Project*, I began to tour libraries and promote the release of the book, showing those attending the tools that are used to document spirit activity and my philosophy for investigating locations. I always include time for the audience to ask questions and of course to tell their own stories. I have stayed long after my lectures have finished to chat with attendees and give my undivided attention to their stories of personal loss and activity they have witnessed. In a way it's also therapeutic talking with a group that accepts the encounters and has been through similar events. As a group of like-minded individuals sharing personal stories, these people know they are not alone in what they are experiencing.

In some cases people talk about loved ones visiting them from beyond the grave. One woman I remember said she felt her husband's presence around her home and at times could feel him lying in their bed. She said at night when she lay in bed and the room was still, she could feel weight pushing down on her husband's side of the bed. I told her not to be afraid of the visits and try to talk to him; he is very much around her. I explained that our loved ones are not gone at all, and in the case of those recently passed, sometimes they stay close to their loved ones to make sure they are ok. This could be to comfort those grieving and to let them know they are still around them. I felt after the woman shared her personal story of loss and afterlife communication, she almost had a weight lifted off her shoulders. The entire room of strangers all shared their personal stories and support for one another; it was a beautiful experience to witness and share with them. To have that deep knowing that death is not the end.

At this one event that I was lecturing at, a family came up to my team and me and began to talk about activity that was currently happening in their home. They explained that it'd been very active for a long time, and their two young daughters had seen the apparitions of a man and little girl. They saw the little girl so much and interacted with her that they had given her a name, "Friendly." The husband and wife had also seen apparitions of the little girl, man and woman and had been chilled to the bone by these ghostly visitors. They wanted a paranormal group to come into the location and see if the activity could be documented. They did not feel that the activity was malevolent but just wanted to see if anything could be captured with equipment. The family was also interested in having a medium's impression of the property and spirits involved. I agreed to investigate their home with my team, the New Jersey Paranormal Project, and help the family understand what was happening and give a voice to the spirits.

I called on the help of a medium whom I had worked with in the past, Maryann Taylor, who has been working cases like this for a long time. I felt that if children were involved, she would be a fantastic fit for this client's case, being a grandmother and amazing with children. I had seen her work in the past, and she has a great way of putting clients at ease. My friend and team member Marci Keck joined us and worked on many of the devices, such as the Kinect SLS camera, Ovilus and Phasmabox, and really contributed to the evidence we would collect that night.

We should begin with the history of the land that the home is located on; the property was once the estate of the Ballantine family that founded the Ballantine Beer Company in 1840. The company was located in Newark, New Jersey. The Ballantine Estate, known as Spring Side, included a beautiful two-story white colonial mansion, complete with a gazebo, a creek, a pond and other outbuildings. This estate was built by Peter H. Ballantine and provided the family with a spacious getaway from city life.

In the latter half of the nineteenth century, this area of New Jersey attracted many wealthy families from New York and New Jersey. It was very common for the wealthy to have a summer residence in the countryside to escape the big city. You can only imagine how many family members and friends enjoyed the comforts of the country life and the hospitality of the Ballantine Estate. There is a carriage house on the property that even predates the Ballantine family on the property; the carriage house has the date inscribed of 1803.

The estate and land were sold and now are the Sedge-field section of Morris Plains, New Jersey. Now what once was the sprawling grounds of the Ballantine Estate is rows of homes and town streets that make up the community. Where the Ballantine family would entertain their guests is now the residential streets where children ride their bikes and life in the suburbs plays out. What attracted the wealthy and the Ballantine family to this area so long ago is still a sought-after community in Morris County.

It's places like this that have so much history and life lived on the properties that could hold residual energy and also still have a connection to spirit. The family who was having the activity was next to the grounds that the Ballantine home was located on. Only a stone's throw away from the family's backyard was the carriage house that dates back to 1803. This area has so much history, and it's no wonder why the family was reporting spirit activity. The activity in this home had been happening with such frequency that the family had grown accustomed to it and had embraced these spirits as an everyday occurrence.

The twin adolescent girls who lived in the home reported seeing the spirit of the young girl they named "Friendly" so often it was like she was another member of the family. The reason they named her Friendly was because she was exactly that: a very friendly and playful little girl. The spirit of the little girl had been seen throughout the house and was the most active spirit in the home.

When interviewing the father, he shared a few interesting stories that he'd witnessed involving the spirit of the little spirit girl. He recalled it was the Christmas season, and he was filming his twins dancing around the room to the music of *The Nutcracker*. As his twins began to perform for their mother and father, he noticed that there was a small orb that seemed to be dancing in a ghostly ballet with the twins. As fast as it appeared and danced with them, it vanished. He went on to tell me that he had an issue making the transfer of the footage from the camera, and unfortunately the video was erased. In the paranormal field, evidence is crucial to documenting the activity happening. Without being able to view this footage, I cannot really give my opinion on the story. What I can tell you is that he was deeply moved by the encounter, and I could tell he was coming from a genuine place.

Another encounter that the father shared happened in the master bedroom in the middle of the night. He awoke to see a little girl standing at the foot of his bed. Being the father of twin girls, he thought it was one of them at the bottom of the bed. He called out his daughter's name and got no response. As this little girl looked at him from the bottom of the bed, she began to lift off the ground and start floating over the bed. His eyes began to follow the apparition as it floated closer to the ceiling and then went through the floor to the upstairs. It was at that point that he could not hold back and let out a scream that woke his wife. It was a surreal experience to witness. I could still hear the excitement in his voice as he recalled the details of that night's encounter. It was at that moment he got to see, face-to-face, what his daughters had been experiencing for a long time, the little girl known as Friendly.

Being intuitive and using the technique of spirit art, I was able to pick up on the presence of two spirits associated with the home. As I sat in my office a few weeks before the investigation was to take place, I let myself open up to the location. Through my mind's eye, images began to play like an old movie film. The first was the image of a young girl, her hair was dark brown, and her hair was long. I noticed her big eyes and soft complexion. Her hair was tied with bows that came down at each side of her cheeks. I would say the child had to be younger than ten years old. I grabbed my pencil and started to do my best to sketch the image of this young child. If I could capture her likeness, I knew that the family could validate if the image was correct and was of the little girl Friendly.

Then I started to write the characteristics of this young spirit. I felt that she came through very playful and at times could be a little mischievous. I felt that she had an abrupt end to her life and was no older than the age of ten. I felt that she might have spent time in a city and the country; she loved this area in life. She was coming to the twin daughters not to scare them but rather looking for a playmate and a connection to children her age. This was what could have attracted her to the home, the fact that two little girls around her age were now living on the land that once was hers.

Richard Moschella Sketch of the Little Girl "Friendly"

Children are very intuitive to begin with; they are

more right-brain dominant. This also helps with their connection to the frequency of spirit. Children are more pure than adults when it comes to culture filters. They haven't been told what to think or how to interpret what they are seeing. They are born with a great deal of intuitive abilities, and as we grow into adults, a shift happens, and we move more to our left-brain thinking. This is more analytical, methodical: language, logic, critical thinking, numbers and reasoning.

Intuitive healer Dr. Kim Peirano wrote "Kids are more susceptible to ghost sightings because they have a much greater sense of awareness than most adults. This leaves them subject to picking up on energies and events that go unnoticed by most. We tend to have a belief that because our kids can't always communicate [their thoughts], that they are unaware or unconscious of what's going on around them. This is anything but the case." I fully agree with Dr. Peirano; children are almost beacons for spirit. How many children have imaginary friends that mom and dad can't see? As they grow up, these invisible friends are talked about less until the day comes when they are forgotten about. This all happens as the child begins to grow up and starts the transition towards left-brain thinking.

There have been countless cases of children recalling past lives and also life before being incarnated. It is documented by many researchers that children recall choosing their parents; you could only imagine the shock when these are some of the first conversations you have with your young child.

In this case I felt that the spirit of the "friendly" little girl was attracted to the twin girls. They saw her and acknowledged her, and this made the spirit of this child happy. She now had kids to play with and interact with around her age. I was also certain that as these twins grew up and entered adulthood, the encounters with the little girl's spirit would be less frequent.

After the image of the little girl faded away, I began to see the image of an older man. He was a large man, and I did my best to write the characteristics that I felt were associated with him. I felt that he had a very strong family ethic, and I got the words lineage and family ties. He was an authoritative type and a very good business-man. When he shook your hand, he had a very firm grip and would look you in the eye. I was able to see money and property also connected to this individual. He really loved being around the children and had an affection towards them. I saw a game of chess being played out; I was not sure if this meant that he was a chess player or was very good at making strategic decisions. I also got the image of alcohol in a glass; he definitely partook in the drinking of spirits. He was an absolute gentleman and very respected. He could be fiery at times but was very passionate about his business. Then the image of a library with beautiful stained wood and books came rushing into my mind's eye. I was not sure if he was a reader or if he was trying to convey that the story of his family has many volumes to it. It could have been his way of conveying that the family history is written about in various books. The image of factories and smokestacks, like a brick city, appeared in my mind. I saw many laborers going into work. The last image was of a lot of land belonging to this gentleman.

Richard Moschella Sketch of the Man

It was a cold January night when Marci Keck, Maryann Taylor and I stood outside in front of the family's home. The moon was starting its rise over the barren trees, and the ground crunched with each step we took over the frozen ground. The husband met us on the front porch and welcomed us into the home.

Once inside the home, I began to set up the devices we would be implementing on that night's investigation. The husband gave Maryann and Marci a tour of the home to give them an idea of the layout of the house. As they were taking the tour of the home, I had a conversation with the wife. She told me that the home had been built in the late '40s or 1950s, and this lined up with the historical information about the land being developed into a community. The wife also told me that she had seen the apparition of a woman in the home and was hoping to get some answers from us about the home's activity.

As we started the investigation, we used the Kinect SLS camera that uses the technology that finds human forms that cannot be seen with the naked eye. The camera also shows the proximity of the invisible figures in relation to your own. This is a great way to sweep a location and look for active areas to focus on. We started in the dining room and quickly mapped a figure that was next to the Christmas tree; the figure was recorded for a few moments before it vanished off the screen.

We made our way upstairs to the bedroom of the twin girls and noticed a smaller shape that was being mapped at the bottom of their beds. This was the room where the spirit of the young girl was seen the most; we all could not help but think as we looked at the stick figure being displayed on the screen, could this be the little girl friendly?

The husband then took us down into the basement of the home, and the SLS camera mapped figures in the darkness of the basement. It is also important to note that the husband was an avid collector of military artifacts. Uniforms of soldiers and flags that were signed by servicemen before they went off into battle were just a few of the items displayed. The walls were lined with photos of soldiers and newspaper articles from the early world wars.

Having items like these could also be another reason for activity in the home. All these items have a connection to spirit and also could hold residual energy. The residual energy will not be intelligent activity but rather like watching a silent movie play out before your eyes. It also could act like a recorded conversation or sound playing over and over when conditions are right. It's something that collectors of these items should always take into consideration. Items can definitely hold energy and bring that energy into your home and also change the energy of the space.

Native Americans were very wary of having their photos taken and often refused. They believed that having their photo taken could steal a person's soul. Other cultures buried artifacts with the bodies of their dead and let them carry them along into the afterlife. Then there are the countless books and television shows that document hauntings associated with haunted objects. I personally feel that items can hold energy and have a connection to spirit and should always be treated with respect and caution.

The husband's collection was beautifully displayed and really showed his sense of pride in his family's service to the country. He also displayed artifacts that had been passed on to him by people who knew of his affection for this kind of subject matter. Items that no longer could be passed down through families had been given to him to keep and preserve. I really felt overwhelmed by the care and knowledge that he had about all the items in his collection. It was no wonder the SLS camera mapped out a figure standing over by a small bar in the corner of the basement. The figure was mapped in an area that also had newspapers from World War II.

With just the walk-through implementing the SLS camera, we knew this was going to be an interesting investigation.

Dining Room Figure

Figure in the Twins' Room

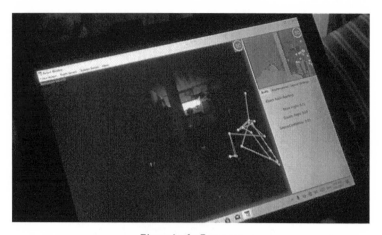

Figure in the Basement

Basement: Two Members Mapped with Figure in the Middle

When our medium Maryann Taylor arrived at the home, she picked up on two spirits in particular, the little girl and the man. She described the little girl as around the age of five and said that she was a little standoffish to outsiders. At times she'd come down the stairs and peek around the banister and observe. Maryann also felt that the little girl might open cabinets and drawers in the home, and the family might find things misplaced. She said the little girl at times could be slightly mischievous; the family immediately confirmed that indeed things like that happen all the time in the home.

Trigger object inside GS2 Laser Grid

As Maryann was doing her mediumship session with the family, our K2 EMF meters were going off the charts. The GS2 Laser Grid was mapping cold spots that would come into the laser grid and then vanish as soon as they appeared. This happened for about ten minutes, all while Maryann was talking about the spirits in the home.

I found the investigation to be really interesting because my team did not know anything about the activity going into the home. The conversation that I'd had when I presented the husband with the spirit art had happened weeks prior and was kept between us. I wanted my team to be kept in the dark about the details; this really helps validate the accounts that are being reported. When all the evidence starts to line up together from the mediumship and devices and pretty much reiterates the same story, one cannot help but feel validated.

We closed out the night's investigation with a spirit radio session and gave the spirits the chance to come through the Phasmabox. At times very clear voices could be heard coming from the tablet that investigator Marci Keck was holding in her hand. There was one point that Maryann, Marci and I could swear we heard our names come through the device.

GS2 Laser Grid on stairs

I have heard investigators' names come through the device in the past at other locations. When we go into a location, I believe that intention is very important, and I always introduce the team members and myself. I want the spirit to know why we are there and that we come with love and respect. So spirits will know the investigators on a first-name basis, and when doing the radio sessions, hearing your name called out is always a great piece of evidence to show intelligent communication with a spirit.

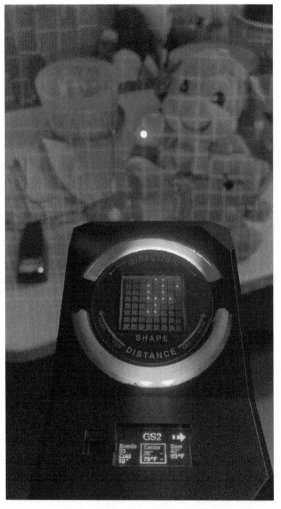

Cold spot moving into the Laser Grid

When homeowners open their doors and allow my team and me into their personal space, it's a great responsibility to not only treat the spirits with respect but all the living people who are trusting the investigators. I only work and surround myself with passionate and educated individuals; it's not only about documenting spirit activity. As investigators and researchers, it's our job to educate the people dealing with the activity.

In most cases, the people experiencing the activity are extremely uneasy and scared of what is going on in their home. My team and I make sure that the clients understand what the activity is and the techniques and devices we use to document it. At times we also explain how the living can coexist with the home's spirits; it's comforting at times when they learn it's a family member who just wants them to know they are still around. Then there are the spirits that are attached to the location from past memories or personal possessions. They mean no harm to the living; they just want to make their presence known.

In this case, the twin girls were also witnessing the activity and saw the spirit of the little girl Friendly, and I felt that one of them could also be sensitive to spirit activity. While interviewing the parents, they went on to tell me that while on vacation in Saint Augustine, Florida, their daughter had seen ghostly apparitions. They were very concerned that she might not know how to handle the situation and the gift of being sensitive.

I made sure at the end of the investigation to provide

the family and especially her with ways to handle the gift of budding mediumship abilities. I went on to explain that you are always in control of the situation, and intention is very important. If you feel over-whelmed, you can certainly tell them to go away and that you want to be left alone. When you want to connect with spirit, setting up an initial way to jump-start communication is a great way to control when you're on and when your off switch is set. I use the simple tech-nique of sitting in the power and letting my energy grow upward and expand; that is how I blend with the spirit frequency. It's truly a simple meditation that works for me. It is very draining and not good to always be on when dealing with the spirit world. You need to be in control of your body and your gift.

This will be a location that we come back and revisit; it's important to see if the activity changes over the course of time. I also have colleagues who specialize in different aspects of paranormal research and will recom-mend that they also work with me to further investigate this location. You would be surprised at how many suburban households have spirit activity. These homes could be your next-door neighbors or even family members. You could even be dealing with the activity yourself; just know you are not alone.

ABOUT THE AUTHOR

Richard Moschella lives with his wife and two children in Rockaway Township, New Jersey. He is the founder and team lead for the New Jersey Paranormal Project. Through NJPP, he enjoys presenting lectures and seminars on the paranormal and his team's investigations. He is an avid reader and researcher of both the paranormal and history.

To learn more about NJPP, visit: http://www.richardmoschella.com

ALSO BY RICHARD MOSCHELLA

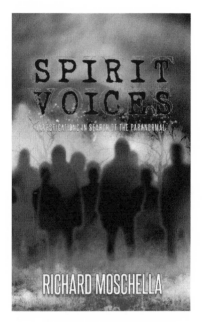

Spirit Voices: Investigations in Search of the Paranormal